DOG IN THE MIRROR IS GOD

DOG IN THE MIRROR IS GOD

A SCIENTIFICALLY SPIRITUAL APPROACH TO TREATING HUMAN AND ANIMAL BEHAVIOUR PROBLEMS

Gaby Dufresne-Cyr

All rights reserved. No part of this publication may be reproduced, distributed, or transmitted in any form or by any means, including photocopying, recording, or other electronic or mechanical methods, without the prior written permission of the publisher, except in the case of a brief quotation embodied in critical reviews and certain other noncommercial uses permitted by copyright law. For permission requests, write to the publisher at the address below.

Copyright © 2018 Gaby Dufresne-Cyr

ISBN: 978-1-7752927-2-2

Editor: Amadea Editing
Photographer: Marilou Léger

Dog in the mirror is God, first edition 2018.

Library and Archives Canada legal deposit LD-2019-2816-2. Bibliothèque et Archives Nationales du Québec legal deposit 450979.

Dogue Shop Publisher
253 Av. Duluth East
Montreal, H2W 1H7
Quebec, Canada

www.dogueshop.com
info@dogueshop.com

For Goulafre…

"Spirituality without quantum physics is an incomplete picture of reality."
— H. H. Dalai Lama

Contents

Introduction 1
   Learning difficulties 1
   Animal behaviour studies 3
Chapter 1: Energy 9
   Energy theories 9
   Einstein's theory 10
   M-Theory is the theory of everything 13
   Universal energy system 16
   Morphic field theory 23
   Reader notes 28
Chapter 2: Emotions 29
   Origin of emotion 29
   Canine emotional language 33
   Emotion as experience 39
   Behaviour problems 43
   Socialization and habituation 46
   Sociability genes 47
   Reader notes 49
Chapter 3: Emotional Projection 51
   Definitions and explanations 51
   Channel transference 54
   Universal energy exchange 57
   Case study: Scooby 59
   Case study: Boreal 60
   Case study: Stick 65
   Behaviour outcome 67
   Reader notes 71
Chapter 4: Modifying Behaviour 73

    Behaviour modification rules 73
    Behaviour modification protocols 75
    The convergence point 83
    Reader notes 88
Chapter 5: Unity 89
    The mirroring process 89
    Recognizing conflict 91
    Case study: Jake 93
    Case study: Ginger 96
    Mirroring technique: Ginger 97
    Step 1: Recognizing conflict 102
    Step 2: Releasing conflict 103
    Step 3: Forgiving conflict 106
    Case study: Marmaduke 108
    Reader notes 111
Chapter 6: Social-Cognitive Learning Theory 112
    Attachment theory 113
    Social learning 117
    Social determinants 118
    Cognitive determinants 120
    Environmental determinants 123
    Reader notes 126
Chapter 7: The Big Picture - SCAT 127
    Separation: Birth of the ego 127
    Unification: Birth of the spirit 131
    Case study: George 137
    The SCAT process in a nutshell 146
    Case study: Albear 148
    Reader notes 153
Chapter 8: Dog in the Mirror is God 155

Energy summary	155
Emotion summary	156
Behaviour summary	157
Unity summary	158
Social-cognitive summary	159
Big picture summary	160
A Scientific/spiritual summary	161
Final thoughts	164
Reader' notes	169
References	171
Author Bio	187

List of Number Figures

Figure 1. M-theory (artistic image by Asher Bilu, 2010)...15

Figure 2. Morphic resonance tunnel……………………….25

Figure 3. Emotional threshold……………………...……….42

Figure 4. Electric currents exchange……………………59

Figure 5. Photo of Boreal…………………………………...62

Figure 6. Interlaced fingers left-right and right-left………75

Figure 7. Operant conditioning quadrants…………………80

Figure 8. Left-gaze bias: Gaby……………………..……..…..83

Figure 9. Social-cognitive triangle…………………….…...117

Figure 10. Human memory……………………………….122

Figure 11. The human-dog bond……………………….…141

Figure 12. Nadhi fingers…………………………………...144

Figure 13. Albear, left gaze bias………………………....…146

Figure 14. Social-cognitive attachment training (SCAT).148

List of Letter Figures

Figure A. Havane..7

Figure B. Albear..186

Figure C. Hariette..189

Introduction

I started writing this book because I felt compelled to discuss our human-animal relationships and the impact we have on each other from a spiritual standpoint. The training method I will present unifies science and spirituality. You might well wonder what one has to do with the other, so I will do my best to explain the concepts as simply as possible. First, let me describe my views about human-animal relationships before we start this self-help adventure together.

I consider my relationship with dogs (*Canis familiaris*) to be a symbiotic partnership. Over the years, I learned so much from the *Canis* genus that I often find myself in deep conversation with dogs and wolves. We tell each other how we feel and what our next course of action is. As a child, my father would stand in awe when I asked our two Great Danes to leave the room with little more than a stare; he would be even more surprised when my dogs executed the request. He just could not figure out how a five-year-old could accomplish such a Herculean task.

Obviously, at the age of five, I could not explain it either. All I knew was that I could communicate with animals and that I had a talent for it. At the age of nine, I told my friends I could speak English, French, and Canine. Almost forty years later, I still joke about it. When people ask me how many languages I speak, I always answer three.

Learning difficulties

A decade later, I attended college and found myself struggling with course content. My English teacher told me she thought I might be dyslexic. She recommended I seek counselling at the school's learning centre. I promptly did this, and the next day, the department tested me for a multitude of learning and hearing disabilities. The person in charge of my case was a wonderful woman who changed my life. Even her name was beautiful: Rose. After rigorous testing, she confirmed the diagnosis and told me I had a learning disability. I was shocked, but at the same time relieved, for the dyslexia diagnosis explained so much. After my initial *I'm-not-dumb-after-all* response, Rose added that I was considered a "nonlinear thinker" with auditory hypersensitivity, letter reversal, and phonemic awareness. An inverted ear canal offers an extra challenge when I find myself in noisy situations.

These issues should have made my ability to learn very complicated, but they did not. I learned to compensate, and my disability went undiagnosed until my mid-twenties. Rose informed me that most dyslexics compensate by emphasizing a skill. I knew exactly what she meant. One of my major coping strategies came from my eidetic memory. A photographic memory proved essential for observing and retaining nonverbal communication signals.

Rose went on to explain how dyslexic folks usually become proficient in a specific field in order to process information. In other words, dyslexics tend to become highly specialized in a particular subject matter to facilitate learning; unconsciously, I had chosen animals, more specifically, animal behaviour as my coping strategy. Still today, every piece of new information presented to me is associated, in one form or another, to the animal kingdom. The technique is so efficient that I eventually learned about quantum physics, universal energy theory, spirituality, biology, and much more.

As it turned out, my eidetic memory served a functional purpose too. Rose and I invented and implemented a new learning strategy. We both thought visual association would be easy to include in my re-learning. She taught me to match the improper word I saw with the proper written word through visual memory. In essence, I would see *boubt,* but trained my brain to read or write *doubt*. When I write, I no longer confuse circular letters, such as a, o, c and the letters b, d, p, g, unless the word is new to my vocabulary; conversely, there are still words I cannot write without cognitively thinking about them.

Rose indirectly contributed to this book by building my confidence and nourishing my desire to learn. My last day at the learning centre was filled with emotion because I felt so grateful for Rose's presence in my life. From that day on, my intellectual nourishment has been fun and limitless. No longer bound by the traditional education system, knowledge and learning in general no longer frighten me, because I can make the connection between animals and any subject at hand. Failure disappeared from my vocabulary, as did impossible, improbable, or impractical. I have tools to understand the world, and have built great things with them.

Animal behaviour studies

In 1997, I left the fine arts program at Dawson College and officially started studying animal behaviour. I attended every college course, conference, seminar, and private school I could find. By 2016, I had received two certificates and a university degree: certified behaviour technician, exotic animal trainer, and family life educator. I am currently working on a second degree in cognitive neuroscience psychology.

Back in 2003, I was lucky enough to be in the right place at the right time. I volunteered to work with arctic wolves at Park Safari African zoo in an experimental socialization program based on Wolf Park's imprinting protocol. This opportunity allowed me to meet animal behaviour specialists Gary Priest, Dr. Erich Klinghammer, Patricia Goodman, and Dr. Raymond Coopinger, who were gracious enough to impart their knowledge. These wonderful people were generous beyond my wildest dreams with answers to my endless questions.

In retrospect, I learned vital lessons: animal behaviour is nothing more than nonverbal chit-chat. When you understand nonverbal language (aka behaviour), talking back is effortless. Finally, when you master dog, wolf, giraffe, or alligator behaviour, you start to think like one, so to speak.

The only downside to learning a nonverbal language is that animals do not repeat or explain what they have just said.

To gain experience, one needs to work with various species of animals and bank endless hours of observation. Luckily, I have had an endless supply of opportunities to develop my nonverbal communication skills.

On an unrelated topic, I took a yoga teacher training course in 2006 to perfect my yoga practice. The programme changed how I understand nonverbal communication. The first change took place in my own body. Yoga taught me to listen to movement, understand my place in space, and respect the mind-body messages I experienced. The practice of *asanas*, or physical poses, taught me how the body expresses emotion through movement, via nonverbal language.

If we cannot express emotions, they are stored in the body. Failure to release your emotions creates dis-eases, or the inability to be at ease with yourSelf.[1] Knowing where emotions are stored in your body is the first step in releasing them. It became apparent to me how animals use their bodies to express and manage emotions. Years of observation made deciphering the canine language easy, but intense yoga training transformed it into an art form.

The second change was more subtle but nonetheless powerful. It happened when a friend and I attended Deepak Chopra's conference in Montreal. Out of nowhere, an imperious man tried to sell us a book called *Disappearance of the Universe* (Renard, 2004). His excessive exuberance about the subject alarmed us, and we both thought he was something of a fanatic, if not a freak. Strangely, though, we did purchase the book that day, because the young man did manage to stimulate our curiosity. The *Disappearance of the Universe* introduced me to *A Course in Miracles* (Shucman, 2007), which changed my spiritual, personal and professional life.

---

[1] Note to the reader: throughout this book, you will note some unusual spellings of certain words: yourSelf, god, re-member, etc. These are quite deliberate and intended as a gentle reminder to reconsider their definition, or serve to place an emphasis on their spiritual, rather than egocentric, meanings.

During the same period, I studied various subjects out of sheer curiosity. In 2005, I researched M-theory in quantum physics and read *Searching for Einstein's God* (Languirand & Proulx 2008). This is when spirituality and science simultaneously merged into one reality in my mind. Dyslexia is funny that way. Strangely, I spontaneously recognized the connection between these opposing disciplines. I understood, at that specific moment, how thoughts, words and actions created what we perceive as reality, and how reality was a construct woven into the fabric of space-time itself. In other words, what we think is real is simply an illusion, a dream with no beginning and no end.

Einstein's vision became clear: god is indeed responsible for everything in and of itself because god IS. How simple is that? Well, it is simple enough to be very complex, yet complex enough to have never existed. I bet you never expected to read about this in a book about dogs! But don't worry: I never dreamed I would write about it either.

To this day, my father still does not understand how I manage animals with little more than a stare. What especially baffles him is that no animal has ever bitten, kicked, mauled, spit at, tripped, or pushed me. Some say I am lucky. But let me tell you: the animal behaviour consulting profession has nothing to do with luck. I attribute my success to education, patience, knowledge, observation, understanding, experience—and dyslexia. I believe animals constantly tell us how we both feel. I simply decided to listen.

> *"Humanity cannot and will not be threatened as a collective. It will always exist, because it is the Superconscious Collective Will of humanity to do so."* (Walsch, 2017).

On a different note, I have included a Reader's note section at the end of each chapter should you wish to reflect or develop the ideas presented in the manuscript. I always find it refreshing to elaborate on certain questions, which makes my books messy and cluttered. I hope you find the extra space is convenient and the text user-friendly for your note taking options.

Figure A. Havane 2004-2016

"You can be anything you want to be
Just turn yourself into anything you think that you could ever be
Be free with your tempo, be free, be free
Surrender your ego be free, be free to your[S]elf."
— Queen, Innuendo, 1991

Chapter 1: Energy

Energy theories

Before we start, I would like to make it clear that quantum physics is not my field of study. As I said earlier, my background is in animal behaviour. Nevertheless, I will explain these complex theories to the best of my ability, because they describe humans and animals as matter moving through space and time, making our behaviours manageable and modifiable.

I hope that you will understand my explanations and the connections made between science and spirituality. I am very aware that not all people understand, or even like, science. At one point in time, I was one of those people. However, to grasp the concepts further elaborated in this book, it is important to grasp the significance of unified energy theory, and how the theory of everything changes our understanding of the world. In this chapter, I will discuss the connection between science and spirituality.

It is truly fascinating to realize just how closely related physics and spirituality are, and ultimately, how they illuminate our work with animals. We will start with simple explanations that should facilitate the flow of the information presented. Here are a few basic definitions:

- Physics is a science that studies the interaction between matter and energy.

- Cosmology is the science of the origin and development of the universe. The Big Bang theory and black hole singularities (McRae, 2017; Neves, 2017) bring observational astronomy and particle physics together.

- Quantum mechanics is a branch of physics that studies small scale and low energy levels of atoms and subatomic particles.

- Quantum field theory incorporates quantum mechanics and the principles of the theory of relativity.

- M-theory is a theory in physics that unifies all consistent versions of superstring theory.

The theories I wish to explain are Einstein's theory of everything, M-theory, and the universal energy system discussed among the followers of Buddhism, A Course in Miracles (ACIM), Hinduism, and other groups not surprisingly, all three theories originate from cosmology. As many scientists study the origins of the world, one concept seems to emerge: matter connects at the quantum level. The kitchen table, you, clouds, the moon, the dog, and everything else in the universe emanates from one driving force. We will explore the many different ideas behind the fabric of matter, in order to grasp these concepts further. At first, it may seem difficult to grasp, but it will become clearer as we go along. If I can understand the ideas presented in this book, so can you.

Einstein's theory

Many of life's questions motivated Einstein to ask: what is the thought of god? What is it like to ride a beam of light? What is the fundamental particle of everything? He kept thinking that there must be a bigger picture, that there must be an invisible force driving the universe (Languirand, 2008; Folger, 2004). If anything, the idea that one unifying force powers all matter drove Einstein to pursue his work. Einstein spent the last 20 years of his life on complex calculations. He thought he would be able to revolutionize physics and ultimately disprove quantum mechanics. Instead, the heritage he left behind helped foster ideas, develop new theories, and discover new particles called *strings*.

To grasp Einstein's theory of everything a little better, one must first know a few facts about the man. As a child, Einstein was rebellious. He did not conform to traditional forms of teaching. He rarely attended school, had poor grades when he did, and questioned every professor who taught him. By the age of eighteen, two educational institutions had kicked Einstein out of school (Isaacson, 2008). By today's standards, the educational system would probably have diagnosed him with Attention Deficit Disorder and prescribed medication for his disruptive behaviour.

But in spite of his never-ending questions—perhaps because of them—Einstein became a widely-known physicist by the age of twenty-five. Like Newton, he fancied the idea of combining theories and applied his knowledge to prove his point. Almost every human being knows Einstein was a great man of science, but very few know that he was a deeply spiritual person, but one who did not believe in organized theology. Einstein thought of spirituality in terms of a cosmic divinity, a kind of universal force responsible for all there is.

> *My religion consists of a humble admiration of the illimitable superior spirit who reveals himself in the slight details we are able to perceive with our frail and feeble minds. That deep emotional conviction of the presence of a superior reasoning power, which is revealed in the incomprehensible universe, forms my idea of God. (Einstein, quoted in New York Times, 1955)*

One might say that Einstein's comprehension of the universe was similar to Native American beliefs (Languirand & Proulx, 2008). Clearly applicable to the human-animal bond and its disturbances, Einstein's concept was that each action influenced the next and that opposing forces ruled the world in a sort of constant dichotomy. To Einstein, the invisible energy that regulated everything had to be an organized force; his favourite saying was, "God does not throw dice."

Many years before Einstein, Isaac Newton merged heaven and earth with his explanation of gravity; the force that holds things in place. However, Einstein's idea that nothing could go faster than the speed of light was incompatible with Newton's law of gravity. Amazingly, Einstein discovered a way to unify gravity and light. He explained that the three known dimensions (height, width, length) and time merged into the fabric of space, which he called the space-time continuum (Isaacson, 2008). This fabric stretches outward, curving and warping; the rounded movement travels at the speed of light to create the force we feel as gravity.

Try to imagine a ball on top of a stretched out nylon stocking; the weight of the ball pulling the nylon down. The ball experiences the pulling down effect as gravity, and the rate at which it takes place is equal to the speed of light. Simply said, when you travel at the speed of light, 186,282 miles per second—or 299,972 km per second—time stops (Farndon et al., 2005). Lightspeed and time stop because the point of convergence between the two forces creates stillness.

The 20th century was a great time for science. This period clarified the four known basic energy theories we now know as gravity, electromagnetism, and the strong and weak nuclear forces. Einstein believed the first two, gravity and electromagnetism, related to one another somehow and he spent the last decades of his life trying to devise a formula to explain it. Although we know him for his *Special General Relativity* and *General Relativity* theories, they were not Einstein's only contribution to science. He produced many theories that improved our knowledge of the world, yet the $E=MC^2$ equation certainly constituted his major contribution.

The formula explains how energy is matter, multiplied by the speed of light squared. To understand this better, imagine a snow globe with the entire universe inside; the universe, that is, the whole globe weighs one trillion pounds. Now, imagine the universe burns to ashes by an internal fire within the globe. According to Einstein, the snow-globe still weighs one trillion pounds, and it does so because matter transforms from one state to another (Languirand & Proulx, 2008). In the snow-globe example, the matter did not disappear, but simply changed from one form to another. By combining these theories, our favourite scientist changed our understanding of the universe and our role in it.

Einstein wanted to provide humanity with a theory of everything. He thought the invisible force that binds particles, thus, transforming them into matter, operated in an organized fashion, making life predictable. Proving that god exists meant finding the equation that explains how particles come together at a quantum level to create matter. Paper and pencil in hand, he worked out numbers, hoping to leave a trail for future researchers. Unfortunately, decades passed before other physicists picked up where he left off.

M-Theory is the theory of everything

String theory is part of a larger theory called M-theory. String theory is very difficult to explain, so I will not spend an enormous amount of time trying to describe a system physicists take entire careers to study and explain. My aim here is to concentrate on the necessary information required for you to understand the next chapters, where we will discuss human and dog behaviour modification.

This hypothesis is the foundation that brings every other theory together, creating a complete view of the universe and the interconnectedness we share. The definition found on the World Wide Web defines string theory beautifully: "Superstring theory is an attempt to explain all of the particles and fundamental forces of nature in one theory by modelling them as vibrations of tiny supersymmetric strings."

Brian Green (2003) explains it beautifully in his book *The Elegant Universe*. He writes that one kind of ingredient, unimaginably small vibrating strands of energy called strings, constitute everything in the universe, from the tiniest particle to the most distant star. We know that matter is made of atoms, and atoms are made of electrons, protons and neutrons. In turn, electrons, protons, and neutrons are made of quarks, gluons, and fermions. But scientists tell us that even smaller particles exist. These infinitely small particles have neither depth nor width, only length. Physicists think only mass constitutes particles. As hard as it is to imagine, a string is one infinitely small particle imperceptible to the human eye or to the strongest microscope ever built. In fact, the actual size of a string is 10^{-33} cm or 0.000000000000000000000000000001 long (Green, 2003).

To put this in perspective: "If an atom was the size of the universe strings would be the size of trees (McMaster, 2003)." Strings are vibrating particles that curl onto themselves (Figure 1). What is even more amazing about strings is that they interact together by splitting and joining, which creates new particles. This coiling produces energy, and like the strings on a musical instrument; each vibration produces different results.

There are two types of strings: open and closed, each attached to a brane.[2] Open strings have two endpoints, while closed strings have one. The open string attaches to the brane by one end and holds matter within itself. The closed string is not attached to the brane, but rather its two endpoints join together forming a complete circle, believed to be the graviton, the basic particle of gravity (Green, 2003).

---

2 A brane is a physical object that generalizes the notion of a point particle to higher dimensions. Branes are dynamical objects that can propagate through space-time according to the rules of quantum mechanics.

Figure 1. M-theory (artistic image by Asher Bilu, 2010).

The scientific method seeks to prove, through research and experiments, that only one fundamental source particle exists. As mentioned before, M-theory is complex to understand. One might well wonder why a person would even mention M-theory in a book about dog behaviour and human healing. The reason is simple: the significance of this discovery is too important to leave out when describing a theory of everything. The scientific description of a universe where everything unifies has significant scientific, behavioural and spiritual implications.

M-theory has another little secret: reality, as we know it, has eleven dimensions: ten spatial and one of time. Rest assured, I am not making this up; the ten dimensions of String and the eleven dimensions of M-Theory are true. Unfortunately, Einstein ran out of time and was unable to explain mathematically where science ends, and spirituality begins; fortunately, however, his curiosity was contagious for a new generation of physicists, whose discoveries abound.

Physicists work hard to try to explain what most people inherently know, namely, that there is only one source to the universe's multitude of matter or absence thereof. We are very fortunate that scientists continually ask questions, formulate hypotheses, and elaborate theories, for our animal behaviour and training profession can only develop if it is based on science, not hearsay or speculation.

Universal energy system

The universal energy system, or unified field, refers to the concept according to which only one guiding force governs the universe; more specifically, we describe the system as being human, non-human animal, vegetable, living or non-living that is non-material. Instead, the classification refers to god, as all matter and anti-matter, solid, liquid, gas…, as one. Simply said, god IS. Books such as *Disappearance of the Universe* (Renard, 2004) and *A Course in Miracles* (Schucman, 2007) tell us there is no need for organized theology, for we are god, composed of all its elements. Our perceived reality is nothing more than an illusion constructed from the mistaken notion that we are a body. Unfortunately, most people misunderstand the significance of this notion.

The majority of humans think their bodies play a direct role in creating reality when in fact, "Our thoughts determine our experience of life, not what happens in it." (Renard, 2006, p.96) or "Projection makes perception" (ACIM, T-13.V.3:5). I will repeat this quotation several times throughout the book because it is important that the concept is accurately understood.

Many Christian denominations refer to the holy trinity: father, son, and holy spirit; however, most of those who subscribe to this doctrine fail to define or explain what spirit is. The universal energy system describes spirit as free will or pure creative potentiality that generates experience through thoughts, words, and actions. This would seem to contradict the mind-body connection, but actually it clarifies it. Spirit is energy, the mind is inner thought, and the body is the outward container that expresses what we call behaviour. The choice between projection and extension determines how the body will experience an event, an idea we will come back to in later chapters.

Meanwhile, each conscious experience you have had or will have is the product of the thoughts that preceded it. Once you express your thoughts through your body, behaviour creates your world, as you know it; this is what the phrase "projection makes perception" means. Unfortunately, there is a drawback, and psychiatrist Carl J. Jung identified it by cleverly naming his hypothesis the *collective unconscious*, that is, the energy that links unconscious minds. Jung was far ahead of his time and was not afraid to think outside the box. He firmly believed that we share a universal thought energy system through past archetypes (Jung, 1936).

> *These ideas resonate with beings in the physical realm who are projecting a similar energetic signature. It is energetic resonance that draws those ideas to them. (...) By simply dropping them [ideas] into the slipstream of what Carl Jung called the Collective Unconscious.* (Walsch, 2017, p. 150)

In order to achieve unity with universal energy, Schucman's *A Course in Miracles* teaches that one must first abandon the idea of separation and embrace wholeness. Consequently, ego is the separation made real; it is the sum of all fears, the negative sum of the collective unconsciousness manifested. Releasing ego will allow a person to achieve enlightenment. Love is god made manifest, the absence of ego, the positive sum of the collective unconsciousness. Ego is the energy created from the belief that separation is real, which, in turn, creates a world of illusion and fear. Most people are unaware of how powerful the ego really is. The universal energy system sheds light on the ego concept. The system explains what we see. What we call reality is simply an illusion. One can say reality is unreal. Once a person dismantles the illusion, the absence of reality is real. Let me explain.

Imagine you are attending a magic show. You see objects disappear, reappear, defy gravity and logic. You do not dispute what you see, for, after all, your eyes seem to confirm what is happening. From your position, that is, from your perception, things appear real; therefore, your mind accepts them as such. Remember, projection makes perception; you want to see, therefore, you do. From the magician's perspective, from his knowledge, things appear very differently. He knows the truth; magic is simply an illusion perceived as real by the sensory organs. Because the magician holds this fact, he cannot believe in the illusion. The magician is the creator, the divine that knows the truth. Spirit, as the creator, never believed, believes, or will believe in magic.

Ego, on the other hand, sits on the edge of his seat in awe and believes everything it sees. Your ego works hard to keep you from discovering life's pretences. The only way for the ego to achieve its objective is to make you believe you are a body, doomed to expire. Ego's *modus operandi* is to create a chaotic world of hate, anger and guilt, with the hope that it can convince you god is dangerous and vengeful. Separation is the goal, and fear is the function by which it occurs. Spirit is the opposite; it is unity and unconditional love. This never-ending dance of opposites: positive and negative, black and white, heaven and hell, is unknown to god. Think about it; if something is complete, how can it be separate from itself?

> *The theory [Madhyamaka] states that everything in life is part of one large 'cosmic flux' of interconnected events. This flux, however, cannot be proven to be real as it, by definition, is also part of the flux. The only way to prove that something is*

> *factually real is to attribute it to something that is complexly separate from all that is 'known' in the flux that is our current existence.* (Dalai Lama, quoted in: awarenessact.com)

Some religions say there is a hell, while others mention hell is here, on earth. Universal energy explains how life, as you know it, is an illusion. god is neither a thing nor a being; yet, it is all those things, for god IS. Think about it: if god created people in his image and punishes them for not being perfect, how does it make him perfect? God is the illusion set free and the re-discovery of who you really are. God is a dog and the nourishment giving life to the dog. Each living being is a representation of the whole, and when you look in the mirror, you see god. So does your dog. Universal energy is the collective unconscious.

As mentioned before, thoughts are pure creative energy travelling back and forth into the collective unconscious, which is shared by all, unlimited in distance, and unaffected by time. Unconsciousness is an information energy superhighway that binds us together, yet we are not conscious of our interconnectedness. As my mentor, Dr. Raymond Coppinger, once said at a conference, "*I don't think dogs are conscious at all.*" I would add, neither are humans. We do not perceive the thought form because it would be overwhelming to contain all the knowledge there is.

This is not a new concept. Remember the branes we discussed in M-theory? Well, Carl Jung also explained how people are connected and able to consciously use the thought superhighway dimension. He theorized that if enough people contributed to the creative potential, ideas would manifest in the physical world. In turn, creativity would nourish the thought superhighway, giving rise to experience.

Many years later, Jung stated there was a difference between the personal unconscious and the collective unconscious (Boeree, 2006). He described the former as the sum of an individual's experiences, while the latter is our species' entire reservoir of experiences. In other words, the collective unconscious is a part of the thought system that is common to everyone; thus, the unconscious function of the brain is better at individuation and self-actualization, termed individualization by Walsh (2005). Think of the brain as the container of thoughts, for the brain does not generate ideas, it simply receives and expresses them.

I like to call the collective unconscious by its original name, the *egregor*. This term, also known as wakeful one, watcher, cosmic energy field, or thought form, has appeared in the literature for hundreds of years (Bernstein, 1998). The ancient Greek word *egrēgoroi* referred to a watcher and possibly originated from the *Book of Enoch*.[3] Another definition of the time referred to *egregor* as an angel, but after researching the term, the best phrase to define it might be "a minuscule biological program," capable of spreading, self-replicating, propagating, and of "parasitizing" people (Bernstein, 1998). The minuscule biological program Bernstein refers to are our genes. The idea that a biological program can link to the creative potential process, reproduce and spread, is, for lack of a better word, remarkable. If genes can create and expand as a creative potential energy form, then the idea of a universal energy system is no longer a probability, but a reality.

When someone mentions a theory of everything, people normally think science, not religion. Yet, one hypothesis will soon become apparent: spirituality and science merge at the point of infinity. For some readers, this statement must sound inconceivable, possibly even blasphemous. Scientists will most likely ridicule and dismiss such a declaration. I totally understand. After all, as a cognitive-neuroscience student, I am a person of science too. How can science and spirituality stem from the same goal you ask? Let us look at the three definitions

---

[3] The Book of Enoch is an ancient Jewish religious work, ascribed by tradition to Enoch, the great-grandfather of Noah, possibly dating from about 300 BC.

that follow, to better grasp the similarities between both doctrines.

> *Should the universe begin a big crunch sort of process, string theory dictates that the universe could never be smaller than the size of a string, at which point it would actually begin expanding.* (Ivancevic & Ivancevic, 2007, p. 36).

> *According to conventional theory, the universe began with a bang from an initial state of zero size, and if it has enough mass, it will end with a crunch to a similar state of ultimate cosmic compression.* (Green, 2003, p. 235)

> *There will come a time when the energies driving the expansion will dissipate, and the energies holding things together will take over - pulling everything back together again. From there the whole process will start over again.* (Walsch, 2005, p. 254).

Like me, you may find these definitions remarkably similar, not to say surprising. The first definitions come from scientists; the third originates from a spiritual book. Some scientists and theologians will tell you that they alone possess the truth and that the other group cannot prove their theory. Spirituality cannot prove the existence of the divine, nor can physics prove the existence of a unified energy theory. But there is another way to think about the science vs. theology dilemma. People cannot *prove* they love their dogs. A person can only theorize that you love your dog based on direct behavioural observations that result from human-dog interactions.

Again, such observations are only possible because our sensory organs send nerve impulses to our brain. Our perceptions make illusions appear real, which in turn confirms our observations. Even with neurological decoding, love remains an unproven concept, for no one can confirm you love your dog, not even a polygraph test. As mentioned above, you cannot see, taste, smell, hear or touch love. You can only experience love through biological functions; but is it true love? The following idea raises yet another question: how do you know what love feels like without sensory or sexual organs?

Cognitive and emotional love is not spiritual love, so the answer cannot be that love comes from my body. The body can experience love, but it does not generate love. The answer to true love is simply "... you know it through and through, balls to bones..." (Silver, 1999). You know what the experience of love is through the body, because of the non-loving experiences you have had in the past. True spiritual love transcends the body. In fact, the body is made of love; thus, the container cannot contain itself.

We gave priests and ministers of religion the task of identifying and explaining our reality. Scientists were made responsible for qualifying and quantifying our reality. We have created two groups to define where we came from and where we are going. Since both groups seem to come up with the same hypothesis, one can only conclude that both are right; god is the universal energy.

In the film *What The Bleep Do We Know!?*, Stuart Hameroff, professor in the Departments of Anaesthesiology and Psychology and Director of the Center for Consciousness Studies at the University of Arizona in Tucson, concludes a discussion about god by saying that "To be interconnected to the universe at its fundamental level is as good an explanation for spirituality as any (Arntz & Chasse, 2004)." He is not the only one who believes that we share a common energy source. Many renowned scientists also speak of a universal connection.

Scientists no longer fear criticism when they discuss spirituality and science as being two sides of one coin. Men and women of science are no longer shunned, ridiculed, or ostracized for having spiritual beliefs.

Unfortunately, in the dog world, things are very different. Only very recently have scientists started to study canine cognition and emotions. So the mention of spirituality within the dog behaviour and training profession is still considered unconventional. Therefore, only a few avant-garde consultants and trainers incorporate cognition and emotional management into their behaviour modification practice.

Morphic field theory

Morphic field is another explanation for universal energy theory. In essence, a morphic field is an energy force guiding a system towards a specific objective, just as branes guide the open and close-ended strings. One could describe this invisible field as an intrinsic motivation: the driving force that pushes an organism to take on a particular form (Sheldrake, 1999). There are several infinite morphic levels, each building on the preceding one. Here is an example of this principle: you are a morphic field made up of various organs, bones, and muscles. Cells constitute different morphic structures made up of atoms and smaller particles. Each morphic level builds on the next. This principle applies to larger structures too.

As an individual, you belong to the morphic field called humanity. If one were to dissect humanity into its various morphic parts, it would look something like this: humanity, nation, country, city, neighbour, family, you, body, cells, and molecules. Each group is connected to the next, building upon itself creating an ever larger organization. This collective group, at whatever level you observe it, creates an energy that contributes to the group entity, or morphic field. In the words of Sheldrake (2005), "Morphogenetic fields are not fixed forever, but evolve. The fields of Afghan hounds and poodles have become different from those of their common ancestors, wolves."

Universal energy is the sum of all matter wrapped into itself, and this cumulative energy source is constantly expanding and contracting. One day, my friend Peter was observing moving particles in his room. He told me that for a moment, the particles seemed to interact together, so he decided to take a picture. When Peter decided to take the photo, he announced his intention through the thought superhighway and the forms responded and expanded. Thereafter, the enlarged visibility allowed him to see the complex structure presented in such a simple form. I initially thought the orbs Peter described were dust particles until I saw them myself.

Another friend, John, took a series of pictures, in which the forms appeared only in the second photograph. John is a skeptic and does not believe in abstract manifestations. But when he saw the images, he was astonished, as he did not believe they were real. People are not the only creatures to have seen morphic fields. Animals observe, stare, hiss, bark, growl at or chase these forms, aka *egregors*. I asked Peter if he thought animals could see *egregors*. Without hesitating, he replied yes, and proceeded to recount events during which his cats would interact with *invisible* objects. I am certain this does not come as a surprise, and most readers and pet owners can recall similar events. No one can say with any amount of certainty why *egregors* manifest themselves. I simply believe they are part of the thought form. Actually, the origin of *egregors* is inconsequential; for, we are all interconnected at a fundamental level.

There is a simple way to understand this concept of morphic fields. In the words of biochemist Rupert Sheldrake (2005): "I propose that they [morphic fields] are transmitted from past members of the species through a kind of non-local resonance, called morphic resonance." (Figure 2) In other words, your past experiences do not define you, but your unconscious past contributes to the reality you choose to experience. Our primitive brains are constantly telling us to be together, to re-member or to connect anew. Unfortunately, our ego impairs our judgment and falsifies our understanding of unity.

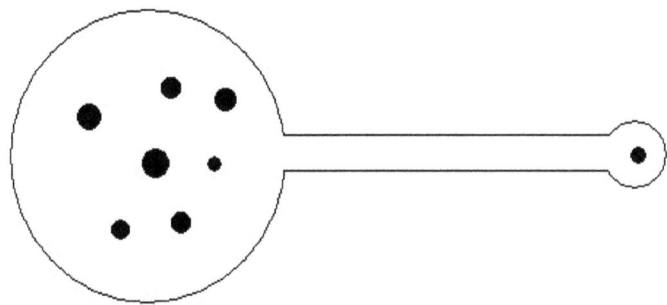

Figure 2. Morphic resonance tunnel.

As mentioned previously, each morphic field has a memory called morphic resonance. In popular terms, we describe the resonance as a constructive force field. A memory that builds on itself through space and time by stretching outward without ever severing the connection. Sheldrake calls this process "morphic resonance (1999)." This projected energy includes an organism's habitual reactions that stretch outward (Sheldrake, 2005). To put it very simply: every particle has a compatible memory field that allows it to evolve into more complex matter. Imagine a cell with an aura surrounding it. Each cell has the capability to transform into every part of your body.

One wonders, how do cells know which structure they should become? They know because of their biology and morphic resonance. Morphic resonance is a morphic field's matrix, which in turn is the building block of a morphic unit. The amazing thing about this theory is its ability to explain telepathy, spontaneous ideas, and déjà vu moments.

> *The morphic fields of mental activity are not confined to the insides of our heads. We are already familiar with the idea of fields extending beyond the*

> *material objects in which they are rooted: for example magnetic fields extend beyond the surfaces of magnets; the earth's gravitational field extends far beyond the surface of the earth, keeping the moon in its orbit; and the fields of a cell phone stretch out far beyond the phone itself. Likewise, the fields of our minds extend far beyond our brains.* (Sheldrake, 2005).

Unlike the heat radiating from the pavement, morphic resonance is a little more than an invisible extension of its physical self. Sheldrake explains it well: "Morphic fields hold together and coordinate the parts of a system in space and time, and contain a memory from previous similar systems." (Sheldrake, 1999, p. 24). Once created, this energy field remains in the space-time continuum, continuously stretching and expanding to incorporate all that is. Ties between morphic field and morphic resonance never sever.

Consequently, these memory-lines crisscross one another and serve as the information web, or thought superhighway (Sheldrake, 2005). The following image demonstrates how this phenomenon occurs between you, your family, friends, animals, and plants. We refer to the process of interweaving memory lines as telepathy or thought transference. Telepathy became popular after World War II. At the time, the army trained people to receive messages from troops abroad in order to plan effective strategies.

Today, few people practice telepathy as a profession, and the average pet owner or caregiver does not understand the intricate nature of the collective unconscious. Although the vast majority of people are unfamiliar with these extraordinary skills, animals have retained their abilities of extrasensory perception and use them frequently. Dogs rely on thought transference and sensory perception to acquire information about their caregiver's location and emotional state. The dog's ability to gain insight into a person's mental state allows him to adapt to the environment, and thus avoid unpleasant situations. Centuries of domestication have created a relationship like no other in the animal kingdom.

Domestic dogs (*C. familiaris*) are the only creatures in the animal kingdom that voluntarily look at a person in order to obtain information regarding a problem (Kubinyi, Virányi & Miklósi, 2007) and to assess their caregiver's emotional state (Guo et al., 2009). Unfortunately, this symbiotic relationship comes at a price.

When social animals live in close proximity, these sometimes demanding living arrangements can cause emotional transference. This negative emotional amalgamation of personalities creates what I call the "*dis* phenomenon": *dis*appointment, *dis*satisfaction, *dis*may, *dis*comfort, *dis*tress, *dis*cord, *dis*order, and *dis*ease. We observe *dis*turbances in the human-animal-bond when communication breaks down; consequently, relationships *dis*integrate, humans become *dis*illusioned, and animals *dis*oriented and *dys*functional.

The only known remedy for the *dis* diagnosis is the "*in* treatment": *in*corporate, *in*terrelate, *in*crease, and *in*tensify. The objective is to create a functional relationship between yourself and the animal you have chosen to share your life with. The result should be a positive exchange based on trust. Before we delve into the complexities of the human-dog relationship, we first need to look at the origin of emotions.

> *There is a metaphysical connexion between the doer and the thing done. Our minds naturally recur from the thought of the one to that of the other.*
> (Hugo, 1853, p. 5)

Reader notes

Chapter 2: Emotions

Origin of emotion

To understand emotions better, one must first look at the structure and function of the brain. Please keep in mind that the following serves as a summary of how the brain functions. A complete cognitive-neuroscience description of the most complex human organ would take not one, but many books. Four parts comprise the brain: cerebrum, cerebellum, limbic system and brain stem. The cerebrum possesses two hemispheres, right and left. Each hemisphere sub-divides in four external lobes: frontal, temporal, occipital, and parietal. The limbic system is located in the middle of the head, aligned with the eyes and ears. The brain stem is composed of the midbrain, spinal cord, medulla, reticular formation, and pons. You can locate the limbic system in the middle of the head, at ear level, descending to the base of the neck (Tortora & Grabowski, 2000).

The cerebrum is the ultimate information-processing centre; each lobe manages general and specific functions depending on the action required. Frontal lobes are responsible for reasoning, planning movement, emotions, problem-solving, learning, thinking and decision-making. We refer to the front part of the brain as the association centre. The temporal lobe controls auditory perception and recognition of stimuli, memory, and speech. The occipital lobes are associated with visual perception. Finally, the parietal lobe deals with incoming messages from the skin and body movement, and registers and processes body sensation, orientation and recognition. The cerebellum influences memory and learning; it also coordinates voluntary movement and balance.

The limbic system is complex, but its main function links emotions and basic motivations. The limbic system controls memory, emotions and regulates basic functions, such as hunger, body temperature and the hormones. The brain stem is responsible for automatic survival functions; it controls reflexes, heartbeat, breathing and arousal (Tortora & Grabowski, 2000). Of all land animals, humans have the largest frontal lobes. Proportions vary greatly from one species to the next; however, the cerebellum/cerebrum ratio remains relatively equal. The major brain difference between humans and animals is the size of the frontal lobes.

Frontal lobe function serves to manage present information based on experience, in order to gain or avoid similar future outcomes. In other words, the human brain loves to generalize. Our organic inner computer has become increasingly good at grouping information. According to the "Brain Top to Bottom" website, repeated actions allow the body to save cognitive function, thus, facilitating faster reaction times when faced with novel stimuli (thebrain.mcgill.ca).

A good example is street crossing. Once we learn the *look-both-sides-before-you-cross* behaviour, we apply it to *every* street crossing situation we face, wherever we find ourselves on earth. Since we do not have to think about street crossing, the frontal lobes have enough processing capacity available, should a problem occur during the traversing.

Variables such as sounds, smells, light-post orientation, or colour disposition do not influence our decision; we know red means stop, and green means go; car or no car is all the information the cerebrum requires to make a choice. The human cerebrum needs very little information to make certain decisions because procedural memory serves to reduce cognitive abilities, which in turn allows for better generalization capacities. The cycle of experience > decision-making > generalization > experience serves to create cognitive space, which Temple Grandin calls *hyper-generalization* (2005). Unfortunately, heightened emotion compromises this process.

Consider crossing the street while talking on a cell phone. If you were to repeat the alphabet to a friend, you would probably cross safely; on the other hand, if your discussion topic is a love dispute, the likelihood of injury increases significantly (Stavrinos, Byington & Schwebel, 2009).

Canines experience street crossing in a very different manner. In reality, dogs are the opposite of people in that they rely less on past experiences to evaluate and decide on the best course of action. From the dog's perspective, problem-solving and decision-making constantly occur in the present. Going back to our street-crossing example, dogs see each street-crossing situation as a separate event. They analyze in detail each corner and base their decision on smell, sound and sight. Dogs take traffic post height and orientation, traffic, and sidewalk design, into consideration.

Based on these factors, we can say that dogs make a somewhat cognitive choice when and where to cross. Left to their own devices, dogs do not learn that green means go or that they should look both ways. In contrast, guide dogs learn the street-crossing skill, but do not generalize the knowledge to *every* street crossing situation; consequently, trainers must treat each event separately and train corners individually. This is an important reason why training a guide dog is so expensive. The increased neuronal activity required for street-crossing requires cognitive abilities, which in turn allows for poor generalization capacities.

One can say that the animal brain over-specifies (Grandin, 2005). If one were to compare the size of the human cerebrum to the limbic system, we would see a two-thirds brain to one-third limbic system ratio. In non-human animals, the cerebrum is relatively the same size as the limbic system. What does this mean? It simply means that dogs are more emotional than humans.

According to Paul MacLean (Kazlev, 2003), the brain is divided into three structural layers, stacked one on top of the other. He termed these three structures *reptilian*, *paleomammalian*, and *neomammalian*, or if you prefer: brain stem, limbic system, and cerebrum. Each part has evolved from the previous, creating a sophisticated emotional management system in which information travels from the lower to the higher level functions, or from the brain stem towards the frontal lobes. This emotional information superhighway extends beyond the brain.

Emotions travel along the endocrine system and spinal cord to every other part of the body (Tortora & Grabowski, 2000). With five hundred million neurons, the intestinal nervous system possesses five times more neurons than the spinal cord; no wonder we get *sick to our stomach* or have *a gut feeling*. Dogs also share our neuronal structure. I have seen dogs defecate when frightened, urinate when happy, regurgitate when excited, or faint when anxious. Emotions might be experienced by various parts of the body but originate in the limbic system.

As mentioned above, the cerebrum receives and manages sensory information, transforming electric currents, commonly referred to as thoughts, into observable behaviour. The difference between human and non-human emotion is a question of complexity, not intensity. Dogs experience basic emotions such as anger, anticipation, disgust, fear, joy, sadness, surprise, and trust; conversely, dogs display conflicting behaviours when they experience more than one emotion at a time. When dogs experience joy and fear simultaneously, behaviour deteriorates. When they experience conflicting emotions, it usually creates intense stress, anxiety, or agonistic behaviour. Humans, on the other hand, can experience conflicting emotions on a regular basis without great emotional distress.

The difference between the two species is not in the actual emotion, but rather in how it is processed by the brain. One could say that the brain functions like your computer: it uses electricity to transform impulses into emotions. The limbic system and the cerebrum collaborate to derive a meaning from the sensory and emotional input, just as computers transform binary input into readable text.

The brain's biological function can be compared to a beautifully engineered supercomputer, equipped with the latest processor. It is capable of accomplishing simultaneous tasks, one of which is interpreting reality. Buddhist philosophy holds that thoughts, words, and actions create reality. Actions, in turn, create thoughts. Consequently, one may conclude that the sum of all thoughts equals one's reality. Positive and negative emotions serve to evaluate experiences generated from reality. Let me illustrate this concept with two examples. A dog has the thought: *I am hungry*. He vocalizes his thought to his human companion with a bark. In turn, his caregiver feeds him. From his action, the dog has created the eating behaviour experience. He has made the experience real; therefore, he experiences satisfaction in the form of need fulfilment and, possibly, joy.

In the second example, a young bear walks in the forest after a fire when he notices an ember. He never saw an ember before. The bear decides to investigate the smouldering piece of wood. The bear moves towards the strange object, huffs and puffs to warn the ember of his approach. He smells the ember and burns his nose. His thought led the way to vocalization and terminated with an action. The negative experience has taught the bear a new reality: fire burns. From now on, the bear will fear fire because he has made an association between pain and embers. His emotional reaction to the physical experience is ingrained forever in his brain. The bear can only change his reality, namely, that fire = pain through a new positive association, which is highly unlikely to occur.

Canine emotional language

Behaviour is the visible result of thoughts and emotions. We call the repertoire of all species-specific non-verbal behaviour an ethogram. Dogs learn their canine language before the age of twelve weeks. We classify canine language into two categories: physical and emotional. The canid physical language includes categories such as agonistic, social facilitation, displacement, investigatory, and so forth. An example of agonistic behaviour is dominance, as shown by raised tail, ears, hackles, etc. Aggression and agonistic behaviour should not be confused; aggression is the expression of the emotion called anger, whereas agonistic behaviours are physical displays of confidence.

A dog can express confidence without being aggressive. Displays of anger include the following aggressive behaviours: agonistic pucker, closed mouth, freeze, immobile tail, lean forward, raised hackles, raised tail, standing on tiptoes, and so on. Aggression is an emotion motivated by nothing more or less than the desire to reduce or eliminate conflict or a competitor. Humans are aggressive by nature, as are most living organisms. Aggression is necessary for survival. Physical language communicates messages from far away, whereas emotional language communicates messages up close. Individuals who learn to communicate behaviours in the right circumstances, and in the appropriate sequence, have a better chance of survival.

Physical and emotional behaviours are not set in stone; behaviour constantly changes to serve a specific purpose or situation. Dogs can experience and express conflicting messages. This happens when roles between dogs are unclear. When canine social structures change, individuals can experience mixed messages. Communication misunderstandings will create confusion and arguments will inevitably follow. As we have discussed previously, the dog's small frontal lobes do not easily accommodate such conflicting messages, which quickly lead to stress and anxiety. Confusion can lead to insecurity and fear. In canine language, dogs express insecurity through submissive behaviours such as ears pulled back, exaggerated body wiggles, an open mouth, a rounded back and so forth.

Fear is an emotion expressed as fearful behaviour: arched back, pulled back lip commissures, lowered head, squinting or soft eyes, tail between the legs, etc. When a human or non-human animal experiences fear, it attempts to remove itself from the fearful stimulus. Dogs cannot display fear and aggression at the same time because they are opposing emotions. When a human or non-human animal experiences anger, it tries to eliminate the stimulus or make it go away. Confident aggression is an offensive behaviour; insecure aggression is a defensive behaviour; insecure fear is a surrender or retreat behaviour. When a conflict is inevitable, dogs must choose between varieties of options: avoid, appease, escape, or surrender. There is no one-size-fits-all reaction, and the response will depend on the individual, the environment, and acquired knowledge.

Whatever the message the animal tries to communicate, if the individual receiving it does not understand the language, it will misunderstand its significance. Communication misunderstandings between wolves and dogs are common. Wolves and dogs share a similar ethogram, but wolves place emphasis on different parts of their language, such as the muzzle grab. Wolves practice the muzzle grab behaviour because it serves to clarify certain social transgressions. Wolves transmit muzzle grabbing from generation to generation because it serves a purpose: to maintain strong affiliations.

Most dogs do not live in groups and have little need for social misconduct clarification behaviours. When wolves interact with dogs, both parties often experience misunderstandings because their language has evolved differently. The wolf might recognize underlying physical signs given by the dog, while certain other signals will remain unfamiliar and difficult to understand.

Simply put, wolves and dogs both speak *canid*, yet their cultural differences create miscommunication. Think of a Brit and a Canadian. We both speak English, yet we struggle to understand certain words and behaviours. When a Canadian stands and waits to enter the movie theatre, we say *stand in line*. When Brits do the same, we say *stand in queue*. Even the word for the place is different: Canadians say *movies* and Brits say *cinema*.

Another example is the human nonverbal greeting. The way we say hello is very different from one ethnicity to the next. The French like to embrace three times when they greet; Asians bend forward without making eye contact; the English embrace once. I returned from London, England recently and can attest to communication misunderstandings. I took me a few trials and a pub landlord to understand what he meant by *loo*, and now I will never forget.

Canid language should always be referred to as conspecific, which means limited to members of the same genus: wolves, coyotes, dogs, jackals, etc. Communication is intraspecific, which means it occurs between individuals of the same species, i.e., dogs. We know animals communicate with each other because we can observe their reactions. I understand what dogs communicate to each other because behaviours displayed in similar situations always lead to the same outcome or consequence. In our dog behaviour jargon, we refer to it as our ABCs: Antecedent, Behaviour, Consequences.

Here is an example: two dogs play in the park. A big Rottweiler bites a smaller Cocker Spaniel. The Cocker yelps, turns around, raises his hackle, lowers his ears, and air snaps at the Rottweiler's misconduct. The Cocker lets the Rottweiler know the bite was a little too hard. Should the Rottweiler ignore the warning, the Cocker has two options: leave or bite harder. The Rottweiler understands the message because he learned to inhibit his bite when he was a puppy. He decides not to push his luck and continues to play with the Cocker. From the behavioural perspective, language is clear, because both animals understand each other. Collaboration and cooperation are essential communication ingredients amongst social animals.

Domestic dogs, coyotes (*Canis latrans*), wolves (*Canis lupus*), and jackals (*Canis aureus*) display different behaviours that result in idiosyncratic messages. Consider the English language again. The dictionary, minus a few spelling discrepancies, is used by English speaking people. In our previous British versus Canadian example, the reason both nations sometimes barely comprehend their interlocutor's pronunciation is that environmental differences have created linguistic drifts. Wolves, the gentlemen of the genus, speak the old version of the Canidae language, while dogs, the bums of the genus, have opted for linguistic drift. Dogs often cut linguistic corners when they interact socially; wolves do not.

Wolves follow a strict communication protocol, and they prosecute individuals who disrespect linguistic protocols.

Here is a good example. An owner walks his dog named Fred when an unfamiliar dog approaches. The strange dog runs towards Fred full speed. Fred dances and prances to greet this newcomer. The owner releases Fred, and both dogs run off to play. The dogs did not exchange greeting behaviours; emotional signals were by-passed; they omitted the compromise signals like play bow, and did not exchange personal information before play. If wolves acted in the same manner, they would severely scold, and possibly ostracize the offending individual for a few hours to a few days.

Animals are born with a set of genetically programmed behaviours compiled and regrouped according to the purpose they serve. We call these chains of behaviours fixed action patterns (FAP), aka mother patterns. Unchangeable and highly ritualized, FAPs serve the animal on a daily basis. However, under environmental pressure, the chain modifies certain parts and evolves into a new sequence. Species practice FAPs and retain new chains if, and only if, they continue to satisfy a survival purpose. As for dogs, they have developed ritualized behaviours that allow them to interact socially, without causing serious harm to other dogs and humans.

Aggression plays an important role in social relationships. Consequently, it is one of the most ritualized behaviours. Aggressive behaviours help individuals create and maintain relationships because they establish an emotional threshold between individuals. Think of a sibling or best friend for a moment. Now imagine you want to send them into a fit of rage. My guess is that you know exactly what to do or say to set them off. You know this because you have done it before and know exactly where the threshold of non-reaction versus reaction is. Social animals do the same. As I said earlier, fear is an emotion devoid of aggression.

Experience, health, size, sexual maturity, temperament, cognition, and the environment influence canine social behaviour. When two dogs meet, social health is the first thing they explore. Individuals will display physical postures of dominance and submission while they greet and exchange personal information. After this initial introduction, the insecure dog tends to submit voluntarily in either active or passive form. Fights occur when animals are of equal confidence, and one refuses to submit. A dominant, aka confident, animal can display aggression but not fear; conversely, an insecure, or submissive, animal can display either fear or aggression, but not both at once. The term *fear-aggression* leads to confusion. The limbic system motivates dogs to display the classical defence mechanisms commonly referred to as the 3Fs: freeze, flight, or fight.

Freeze is the conversion point between flight and fight. Flight, or the runaway strategy, is normally the favoured responses. Fight is normally a last resort response option because it requires an extreme amount of energy and excellent communication skills. When an insecure dog decides to fight, a hormonal shift must occur in his brain to allow an aggressive response. The release of fight hormones such as epinephrine, acetylcholine, serotonin, norepinephrine, arginine-vasopressin, testosterone, etc. is essential for survival (Siegel, Roeling, Gregg, & Kruk, 1999). The change in the body's chemistry allows the dog to exhibit aggression, which, in turn, allows him to fight (Abrantes, 1997).

Let me take a moment to clarify a myth. You will never see a dominant dog, wolf, or other canids, grab an opponent by the scruff of the neck, pull him down to the ground, and hold his adversary until he submits. The alpha roll described on television is a myth. Canids do NOT display this behaviour because it does not exist in the canine ethogram. Dogs submit voluntarily, or they fight. When dogs fight, the conflict is usually brief and injury free. Every living organism strives to die another day. The pin-down behaviour is indeed a myth.

Wolves greet and exchange personal information before they establish social boundaries; thereafter, if all bodes well, wolves establish social affiliation. Canines display physical behaviours that allow humans to decipher their language; however, body postures have limitations, for they fail to express the reason behind the display of a particular behaviour.

The average pet caregiver understands dominance, submission, fear, and aggression postures; however, messages lack subtle variation and meaning when we try to decode them based on only four categories.

Nonverbal communication is pointless without emotion; just think of how omnipresent emojis have become. Interpreting body postures without considering emotions is the equivalent of using vocabulary without punctuation. *When you read this sentence without punctuation it becomes very hard to make sense out of what you are reading because your eyes get tired your brain becomes exhausted and you feel lost confused and frustrated so think of your dog when he talks to you in the future it will help you understand what he goes through on a daily basis when you speak to him.*

The foregoing "sentence" helps to demonstrate how demanding language can be when certain elements are incomplete or absent. Imagine the following scene: a woman, Dana, meets her girlfriend, Ruth, in a park. Dana approaches Ruth, extends her arms out to embrace her, only to realize that her girlfriend has been crying. Dana asks what is wrong, but Ruth responds that everything is fine. Science would agree if you said Ruth was lying. Actually, seventy-nine percent of people believe nonverbal language over verbal information (Beebe, Beebe, Redmon, and Geerinck, 2007). The reason is simple. The conscious part of our brain can easily identify nonverbal communication. Unfortunately, the part of the brain responsible for decoding and understanding emotion is the unconscious part.

Emotion as experience

According to Charles Darwin (1872), the basic emotions expressed by animals are anger, anticipation, disgust, fear, joy, sadness, surprise, and trust. These simple emotions have originated and evolved into social survival mechanisms, so to speak. Without emotions, basic or complex, animals would not live very long. Emotions described by Darwin might be easily recognizable in dogs; however, one has to remain objective. We know dogs communicate their emotions through subtle physical signals and emotional displays. When dogs perceive unavoidable conflicts, they resort to distance-increasing signals.

The goal is to put distance between yourself and your opponent. Distance-decreasing behaviours serve to shorten the gaps between socially attached individuals, thereby solidifying social bonds and bringing individuals closer together. It may sound strange, but dogs cross the line into conflict often, for the act of doing so allows them to express their emotions and confirm attachments.

My psychology professor shared an interesting observation that illustrates my point. She told me how she immediately knows if a couple who are consulting her for marital issues will reconcile or not. In her experience, couples who argue and fight while they enter her office for their first sessions are more likely to work through their problems, in contrast to those couples who never speak to one another. I have noticed the same in dogs. Arguing dogs share a healthier relationship, for dogs who address the emotion that triggered the dispute resolve it.

To understand this further, let us briefly look at the cerebrum and its neural transmission mechanism. Two types of neurons make up the brain: excitatory and inhibitory (Tortora & Grabowski, 2000). Neurons are composed of a soma, dendrite, axon and axon terminal. The synaptic cleft is the space between an axon terminal and a dendrite. Synaptic vesicles fire neurotransmitters where they move from the pre-synaptic (axon terminal) neuron to the post-synaptic neuron (dendrite). Neurotransmitters cannot stay in the synaptic cleft; they must attach to the post-synaptic receptor, or the synaptic vesicle recaptures them.

The role of neurotransmitters is to either excite or inhibit neurons. Post-synaptic receptors decide if neurotransmitters will excite or inhibit neurons; consequently, when a person or dog is under stress, the neurons fire faster, not more strongly. Neurotransmitters proportionately increase in volume, not in force. Simply put, a strong stimulus does not make a dog's reaction more intense; it makes it last longer. Consider beer for a moment. The percentage of alcohol in beer remains the same no matter what quantity you possess. One litre of beer and one thousand litres of beer have the same percentage of alcohol per volume. The major difference between one and one thousand litres of beer is the amount of time it will take you to eliminate the effect from your system.

Neurons need time, and lots of it, to recover from a positive or negative emotional situation; therefore, emotional stress prevention remains the best management option. If conditioned emotional responses (CERs) become chronic, canines will experience an increase in cognitive dysfunction. Once emotions are conditioned, they rarely subside on their own. Unable to process information cognitively, dogs will cease to act, and start to react as CERs increase over time (Figure 3). Chronic emotional stress in dogs quickly becomes a *stress-be-gone* situation, so to speak. Dogs will work hard to make the stimuli go away when humans fail to offer a stress-free environment. The problem with *stress-be-gone* situations is how dogs make stimuli go away; dogs try to stop stressful situations by growling, baring their teeth, or biting.

I have concluded from my personal cases, observations, and notes that the vast majority of dogs who live in dense urban cities suffer from some form of chronic emotional stress. However, not all is lost. We can help dogs reduce CERs and find emotional stability once again. We will cover this topic in the chapter on behaviour modification.

Emotions also serve a spiritual purpose. They teach us the difference between knowledge and experience. To know joy and to experience joy are two very distinct things. We do not know precisely what dogs experience when they are angry. However, we can hypothesize that their experience is similar to ours, based on our emotions, and how they make us feel. We can infer that individuals who are sensory deprived from birth understand the distinction between knowledge and experience. For example, visually impaired people know that purple is a colour, but they will never experience the colour emotionally.

Without auditory input, people will never cry when a soft melody is played, or get angry when the neighbours play punk rock at three in the morning. The emotional experience of music remains as pure abstract knowledge, without the sensory experience. That said, there is always a way to get around sensory input problems.

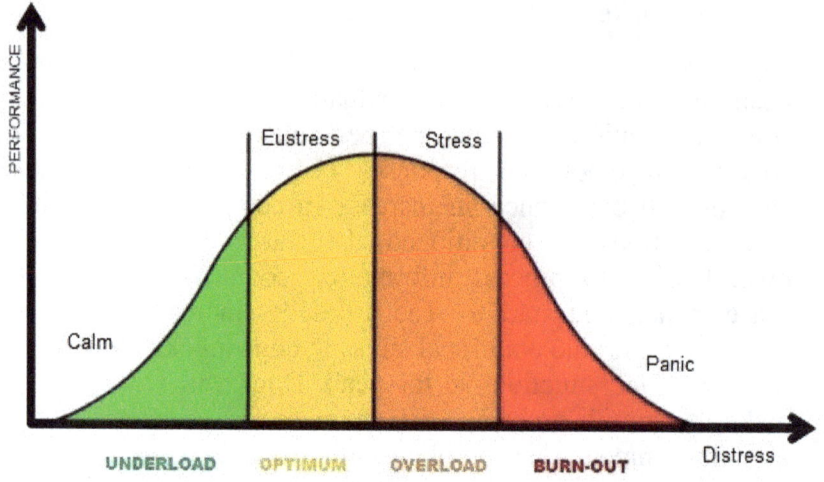

Figure 3. Emotional threshold.

Brains are equipped with special neurons that generate empathy; we call them mirror neurons. In human culture, empathy is a highly valuable trait because it helps us stay alive. As children, we mirror, or copy, what adults eat, do, say, feel because it serves an evolutionary purpose. Without mirror neurons, we cannot empathize. Lack of empathy leads to group dysfunction, chaos, group division, and possible death; therefore, when people see displays of human emotion in animals, we conclude it is a natural and normal process. Case in point: try yawning when your dog looks at you and wait (Hare & Woods, 2013). Most dogs will yawn within 90 seconds. I am sure the vast majority of you yawned as soon as you finished reading this sentence. That is very normal.

Humans relate to one another through mirror neurons and their ability to mimic emotional experiences (Bekoff, 2007). So does the family pet. Unfortunately, true anthropomorphism is an insidious, sneaky, and dangerous trap that often comes disguised as empathy. Anthropomorphism is not empathy; anthropomorphism is projection.

> *The escape from darkness involves two stages: First, the recognition that darkness cannot hide. This step usually entails fear. Second, the recognition that there is nothing you want to hide even if you could. This step brings escape from fear.* (ACIM, 2007, T-1.IV.4:7)

Behaviour problems

A behaviour problem may not be what you think. If an animal digs holes in your backyard, barks at the mailman, protects its food bowl, chases cats or squirrels, growls, or shows its teeth, these are not problem behaviours. While such normal species-specific behaviours can be a problem for caregivers, they are not behaviour problems for the dog.

What we, as professionals, call behaviour problems are clinical issues that prevent the animal from exhibiting normal behaviour, that is, from functioning normally. A clinically aggressive dog will be unable to function because of high levels of reactivity; for example, it exhibits high stress, is constantly alert, barks, lunges, fights, is untrainable, etc. Clinical aggression is taxing on the body (Overall, 1997).

Clinically fearful dogs will also display dysfunctional behaviours and have extremely low levels of activity and reactivity: they may starve, urinate or defecate inappropriately, refuse to play or walk, etc. Vocalization is another common behaviour problem. Barking is a normal dog behaviour. However, while many pet caregivers consider barking to be a behaviour problem, professionals consider barking to be a problem only when it becomes clinically obsessive.

From the human perspective, the difference between normal and abnormal behaviour is tolerance. For example, I have a very low tolerance for barking. When my dog vocalizes because a noise surprises him, he immediately looks at me, and I say *silence, please*. On the other hand, many of my clients do not seem to mind their overzealous barkers. It is a question of patience, tolerance, and perception.

As mentioned before, a non-clinical behaviour problem is anything that irritates a person, but does not cause a problem for the dog. Conversely, a clinical behaviour problem is any action that impairs the animal's normal physical, psychological, and emotional well-being. One need only search video sites such as YouTube to find examples of clinically ill canines. Internet videos and certain television shows present such problems as funny and entertaining. Speaking personally (and as a clinician), there is nothing amusing about a psychologically troubled dog attacking his hindquarters for emotional relief.

Normal behaviour can be equated with the emotional expression of learned associations plus (+) needs satisfaction or dissatisfaction. Behaviours are always observable, measurable, quantifiable and qualifiable. Behaviour problems are abnormal expressions of conflicting emotions and biological dysfunction. These impaired and disruptive responses normally escalate over time, both in intensity and frequency. My dog is hungry (needs to eat) + my dog eats (is satisfied) = positive experience.

Put more simply: my dog is happy. My dog is hungry (needs to eat) + my dog does not eat (is dissatisfied) = negative association, or, my dog is unhappy, stressed or anxious. Troubled dogs develop behaviour problems when the association between need and satisfaction results in negative outcomes, or when biology malfunctions. In simpler terms: the dog feels good or bad, either physically and emotionally, through associations. We normally consider behaviour to be negative when the brain is biologically predisposed to *hyper*active or *hypo*active neural activity. Rarely do we consider behaviour normal when a dog presents neural or hormonal dysfunction.

Both positive and negative outcomes can result from reinforcement or punishment. In Chapter 3, under the heading "Behaviour modification," we will discuss the principles of conditioning. For now, however, one simply needs to remember that dogs can make either positive or negative associations. When animals seek to satisfy their needs, they evaluate the possible outcome, based on how pleasant or unpleasant the consequence will make them feel. For example, a dog needs physical proximity, but if the owner disciplines the dog harshly for jumping on the couch, the dog slowly starts to fear social contact.

You can see this phenomenon in domestic dogs and throughout the entire animal kingdom. Dogs often exhibit inappropriate approach/avoidance behaviours towards people because they have had bad experiences resulting in negative associations. Remember, dogs can learn, but they have great difficulty assessing situations based on past experiences in order to predict future outcomes.

Imagine the following scenario from the human perspective. An owner goes to work in the morning and leaves the dog alone all day. Shortly after the owner's departure, the dog becomes anxious and destroys the furniture. The owner returns, sees the damage and punishes the dog for its bad behaviour. Now imagine the same situation from the dog's perspective. The owner leaves, the dog gets anxious and destroys furniture to relieve stress. The owner comes back home. The dog is happy and greets the owner. The owner punishes the dog because of the destroyed furniture. The dog now makes the following association when the human enters: physical need (touch) + emotional need (social) = pain.

If only it were that simple. In reality, this is where it gets complicated. Canines must sort through a lot of human verbiage to find words they recognize, and that takes time. Consequently, the dog must interpret the owner's nonverbal language to determine a meaning. Not surprisingly, interspecies miscommunication and confusion create most behaviour problems. I often tell my clients that I have not got around to writing a dog-to-human/human-to-dog dictionary yet, so be patient. Jokes aside, it can get very frustrating for both parties, when communication channels fall apart. The best way to avoid behaviour problems is to expose dogs to various stimuli. Active socialization during the critical period of social development serves to prevent behaviour problems; but more specifically, it helps humans understand their puppies' language as they develop.

Socialization and habituation

Socialization is the process by which a dog acquires verbal and nonverbal language, practices these new communication tools, and utilizes them to establish and maintain social relationships (Scott & Fuller, 1965). The most critical part of the socialization period in domestic dogs occurs between the fourth and eighth week. This period comes to a close in the eighth week, ends around twelve weeks, and is completed at sixteen weeks (Freedman, King & Elliot, 1961; Scott & Fuller, 1965).

Within the socialization phase, we find a habituation period. Habituation is the act of acclimatizing to stimuli such as sounds, smells, movements, and touches. Habituation lasts a little longer than socialization and ends at approximately the sixteenth week. When poor socialization and inadequate habituation to environmental stimuli occur during the critical period of development, they cause behaviour problems in dogs. Dogs that do not experience socialization or encounter various stimuli during the critical period of development normally display social fear. In many cases, they react aggressively towards unfamiliar people and stimuli. You can now see why adopting puppies born and raised in a rural environment is a bad idea. There are simply not enough stimuli and social opportunities to experience.

Sociability genes

Social animals are born with a predetermined level of social attachment and resilience. The majority of people believe sociability is genetic, yet science could not provide evidence to support their claim, until recently. Scientific research that explores sociability genes is relatively new, as compared to behavioural research. The studies began in the 1980s and recently intensified. In 1997, Dr. Anthony Wynshaw-Boris from the National Human Genome Research Institute discovered a gene responsible for social behaviour in whiskery mice (*Mus musculus musculus*), a highly sociable laboratory mouse best known for its whisker cleaning behaviour.

What the scientists called the *"dishevelled gene"* came from an altered species of mice. The researchers found three versions of this gene, *dishevelled 1, 2* and *3*. In order to understand the role of this gene, Dr. Wynshaw-Boris removed dishevelled-1 from the whiskery mouse. To his astonishment, the mouse grew normally. However, once the mice reached adulthood, he noticed the mice groomed their whiskers poorly. The team wondered why. They observed the animals closely and noticed a decrease in their social interactions. They also noticed that the mice found it difficult to eliminate exterior stimuli and concentrate on one specific stimulus. Against all expectations, the genetically modified mice interacted, nestled, slept and groomed less. Clearly, something had changed in the group. The mice had become asocial. Was removing the gene responsible for sociability? The conclusion of the study was not clear. However, the facts demonstrate that social interactions were gone, their behaviours had changed, and this gene was somehow responsible (National Human Genome Research Institute, 1997).

A few years later, in 1999, Dr. Tom Insel and Larry Young, from Emory University, published research conducted on prairie voles (*Microtus ochrogaster*). The goal of the study was to discover the mechanisms of a hormone responsible for social attraction and intimacy: vasopressin. This time researchers created a social mouse by inserting the gene from a species of prairie vole known for its sociability and fidelity. Researchers injected the hormone vasopressin into a species of polygamist and asocial mice. The new transgenic species demonstrated the same social and gregarious behaviour at the prairie voles. It was the first time scientists identified a gene responsible for social behaviour (Insel and Young, 1999). Recent research also points to a gene, or possible series of genes, responsible for socialization. In their research, (Persson et al., 2015) concluded: "Heritability estimates of the Principal Components scores revealed a significant genetic contribution to the behaviours involved in test interactions as well as social interactions." (p. 342).

They also have cardiovascular problems, particular physical and facial characteristics, and mild to moderate intellectual disabilities. Adults who suffer from this disorder demonstrate unusual capabilities for language, despite their reduced cognitive abilities. Researchers discovered that children with Williams syndrome got very high marks when administered sociability tests. These tests included the ability to recognize faces and names, the desire to please, empathy and social attraction. In the same study, researchers discovered that one child retained one of the twenty genes usually missing. After this discovery, the scientists administered a new behavioural test to the little girl. Surprisingly, she did not exhibit the typical socially extroverted characteristics which other children affected by Williams usually demonstrate. Instead, she was rather introverted, lacked sociability and was fearful of strangers.

The results implied that the presence of this gene altered the hyper-sociability typically observed in people with Williams syndrome. Researchers concluded the study by saying they were not sure if the gene involved in regulating social behaviour applied to the general population or simply to those affected with Williams (Bellugi et al., 2007).

Reader notes

Chapter 3: Emotional Projection

Definitions and explanations

Before we jump into emotional projection, I want to define a few terms, so you do not get lost in the following chapters. I will start with a few basic terms and then combine them to form new concepts that will lead us to emotional projection. The following definitions come from Oxforddictionaries.com unless specified otherwise.

- Empathy: the ability to understand and share the feelings of another person. Anthropomorphism: the attribution of human characteristics or behaviour to a god, animal, or object.

- Projection: a form of defence in which unwanted feelings are displaced onto another person, where they can appear as a threat from the external world (Britannica.com).

- Extension: A part that is added to something to enlarge or prolong it; the action or process of enlarging or extending something.

Emotional projection is the psychological process by which people unconsciously assign emotions they think they have, wish they had, or do not know they have onto animals, in order to alleviate guilt or other negative emotions. Remember, projection creates perception. Emotional projection also includes the projection of positive emotions. Emotional projection serves to make dogs responsible for their negative life experience; obviously, this is not a conscious process.

To better illustrate the concept, think of a boomerang. You throw a boomerang, and it spins around, comes back, and hits you on the head. Here is a human example: Peter tells Paul, I'm soooo tired of hearing John complain all day long. He drives me crazy with his stupid comments. In the example, Peter is a little frustrated with John's rants, when in reality, Peter complains all the time, but unconsciously cannot tolerate his own behaviour. Peter makes John responsible for how he feels; that way, Peter does not have to deal with his own negative complaining behaviour. In the example, Peter emotionally projects and John anthropomorphizes. Emotional projection is a form of anthropomorphic empathy gone wrong.

Empathy is the process by which a person can relate to another because of our mirror neurons. Anthropomorphism is slightly different for it ascribes human characteristics to objects, events, or other living organisms without truly believing in the idea. People often confuse projection and anthropomorphism because of the outward attribution of emotions. Let us sort through anthropomorphism and emotional projection.

The statement my plant dances in the wind is not anthropomorphic in nature, for plants do not dance, they move. In this case, the person simply used the wrong terminology to explain an action. People who empathetically anthropomorphize, or emotionally project, attribute emotions outwardly into and onto the world and people in it. The sentence my plant hates to dance in the wind is anthropomorphic, and would only be considered emotional projection if a person believed the statement or became angry at the plant for moving.

The difference between emotional projection and true anthropomorphism is subtle, yet important. The former originates from the unconscious, whereas the latter is easily identifiable as an anthropomorphically conscious description. Here are a few examples. Can you identify which sentences are true emotional projection or anthropomorphic in nature? Take your time and think it through. It can be difficult to differentiate both processes from one another.

"My dog Rex hates to sleep in on Saturday mornings. He's angry all day if he misses his dog chasing opportunities."

"Last week my dog Rex destroyed my favourite chair because I went to the movies with my friends Jane and Sally. He's a spiteful creature."

"My dog Rex shakes hands when he wants something. He will even ask the cat to help. Obviously, the cat refuses; he has other plans up his sleeve."

The third sentence is anthropomorphic, for it describes actions exhibited by the dog and cat from a humanistic point of view. Sentence 1 and 2 relate to emotional projection because the humans ascribe their own negative emotions to their animals. Dogs do not seek revenge or philosophize about being spiteful. Dogs function under one simple and straightforward rule: stay alive. I might burst your bubble here, but dogs do not care about how we feel unless it serves the rule or avoids breaking the rule. My dogs do not wake me up in the morning because they love me; rather, they wake me up because they need my opposable thumb to open the door for bathroom duty. If my dogs loved me, they would let me sleep until eight, but that is beside the point and a tad anthropomorphic. I wanted to see if you were following along.

Let me summarize before we move on. The following picture is a screenshot of a video that often circulates on social media. In case you have not watched it, the film shows the dog with her puppies as the rescuer takes her into its care. A few seconds in, the dog looks as if it is shedding a tear, and the woman, in a soft tone, says, *you don't have to cry, you're going to be ok*. Biologically speaking, dogs cannot cry. The discharge that came out of the eye is due to a variety of medical conditions.

Channel transference

Universal energy theories describe all matter as one force, connecting us all. This interconnectedness creates communication channels that remain undisrupted by space or time (Arntz & Chasse, 2014). Emotional projection is simply the inevitable transfer of information between channels; for at the quantum level, emotion is little more than energy; electric currents interpreted by our brain. Knowing this, a few questions surface: Why do humans project emotions? What purpose does it serve? Do animals project their emotions? One could describe emotional projection as empathetic transference. People project to feel better about themselves because it relieves guilt. Projection is a defence mechanism serving to protect the ego from perceived attacks. In other words: you might attack me; therefore, I will attack you first. To explain the process further, imagine the following situation from the clerk's point of view. A woman in a store disputes a charge for a product she did not purchase and concludes the transaction.

> Clerk: (*sighs impatiently*)
>
> Woman: *No need to lose your patience!*
>
> Clerk: *You are an unpleasant client!*
>
> Woman: *What bug bit you today?*
>
> Clerk: *You bit me, and you're about to get squished!*

In today's jargon, one might say *that escalated quickly*, and it would be right. Conflict always escalates rapidly. From the clerk's perspective, the woman is attacking him; therefore, he feels the need to defend himself and strike back. Unconsciously, he thinks *you are not like me; you are bad. I am good, and since I'm better then you, I need to get rid of you.* This is far from the truth. In reality, the clerk experiences separation at the unconscious level and projects his negative emotions outwards. The woman experiences the situation as a confrontation and counter-attacks. The match is set and the clerk, afraid to lose, formulates his final attack. His aggression, mild as it may be, is a symptom of his own inadequacy.

Remember, projection is the process by which we assign emotions or characteristics we would like to have or hate to have. In the above example, the clerk lacks self-confidence and projects his shortcomings onto the customer. When the clerk tells the woman she is unpleasant, he unconsciously sends himself one of two messages: the clerk wishes he were confident or he is sometimes unpleasant and does not like that about himself. Unfortunately, projection is a two-way procedure. When people interact, both parties project their emotions outward. The process stops if, and only if, one person consciously recognizes the projection and does something about it. We will discuss this further in the Mirror Effect section; for now, we will continue with projection and its energy source, fear.

The most interesting feature of emotional projection is unquestionably the force that drives the process. Just like a battery's positive and negative polarity, emotions have a positive and negative charge. This probably comes as no surprise. What may seem more surprising, however, is that only two emotions are responsible for projection: love and fear. Whichever way you put it, every known emotion is a reflection of one or the other. Love is the positive force that guides the projection inward in search of the answer to the question *who am I?*

In essence, to love is to be whole; therefore, love is *holy* because it extends outwards, containing everything. Fear makes people feel empty. Fear is the negative force that drives the projection outward in search of answers to the questions *who am I?* and *who are you?* Ego projects fear into the world, which in turn creates the illusion that you are separate from others. Ego constantly tries to convince you the outer world is the cause of all your inner suffering; consequently, ego must eliminate or sabotage your own body. Another distorted perception ego would like you to believe is that acquiring material things, people, titles, roles, animals or plants, will fill the emptiness that separation creates. Ego is separation made manifest, and to feel separate from the whole is in fact unholy.

> *All fear is ultimately reducible to the basic misinterpretation that you have the ability to usurp the power of God. (ACIM, 2007, T-2.I.4:1)*

When we start to experience fear over long periods, our ego creates the projection defence mechanism. From a spiritual standpoint, ego is born out of a single thought; the idea that separation from the whole is possible. One believes this so blindly that the body actually becomes the physical representation of this idea. The association between mind and body develops in childhood and consolidates during adolescence. The famous psychologist Erik Erikson called this period Identity vs. Role Confusion (Kroger, 1996). We create our identities from the union of mind and body.

Consequently, we experience the outer world as real. We now know the world is an illusion; life, in all its shapes and forms, is simply an outer projection of one's inner perceptions. Death is the ultimate concept of separation, and the ego's objective is to achieve the end-of-all-things by any means necessary. In psychology, we refer to this term as the self-fulfilling prophecy, or self-sabotage. More often than not, ego succeeds and perpetuates the idea of separation. When it is separated from the whole, the ego becomes the only voice one can hear. The voice of ego can get very loud and disruptive.

So, why do humans project their emotions? People unconsciously transfer their emotions to relieve fear and the symptoms of fear: guilt, doubt, anxiety, anger, frustration, sadness, jealousy, etc. Doubt in god's love, guilt for believing separation is real, and the fear that an angry god might punish me are good examples. People who blame family, friends, colleagues, or strangers for their inadequacies transfer their guilt onto others to feel better. Since it sometimes works, people continue to believe that separation is real. I know we discussed this topic earlier, but repetition generates recollection, so bear with me.

From the unconscious projection action, people begin to think that attacking others mentally grants them power over god. Thus, to control others leads the ego to believe it defeated god and has taken its place. Having done so, people unconsciously believe they have defeated death and gained control over life. Obviously, this is a distorted perception. Reality, as we know it, is simply a different level of dream. A nightmare in which most humans dream of a world filled with disappointment, injustice, disease, war, and death. Unable to awaken, people think they are condemned to eternal darkness, and death serves as a constant reminder. The debilitating emotion associated with loss of life ends by controlling human action and rendering people incapable of fulfilling their true purpose. The void leaves an intense feeling of loneliness and isolation.

Nothing seems to alleviate the emptiness humans have grown accustomed to feeling. For the vast majority of people, their distorted version of the world is so grand; they have come to believe the dream is true, therefore real. Fear has taken over, panic has set in, and the only feasible outcome is to blame others. Thus, the projection cycle continues and engulfs dogs in the process.

Universal energy exchange

As mentioned in Chapter one, your morphic field is composed of yourself and your family. But when you acquire a dog, something strange happens. The dog leaves his morphic field, without breaking away from it, and becomes part of yours, creating a new morphic field. Once this union is accomplished, the dog becomes an integrated part of the new field and shares its energy and memory. The dog literally connects to, and shares, your energy current. Using a simple analogy, allow me to demonstrate the principle behind the theory.

To create electricity, we need an equal part of the positive and negative energy, in our case, positive or negative emotions. Imagine yourself and your dog as batteries: in the best of worlds, the exchange between two energy points occurs according to the (+/-) (+/-) convention and creates a functioning system (Figure 4). However, from the point of view of the relationship, if the exchange is mostly a one-way deal, in the positive or negative convention (+/-) (-/+) or (-/+) (+/-), the balance is disrupted. Overall, our dogs give us unconditional love, and in return, we project our emotions such as fear, frustration, or anger and create double negative or positive conventions.

Now, imagine you are a rechargeable battery. After prolonged use, you become weak and cease to function; you need to recharge; you look for the nearest available source and discover no available supply. Because of ego, people have forgotten the purest energy source lies within, in the form of love. Consequently, some pet caregivers unconsciously use animals as their charger. Inequitable transfers of energy create disrupted fields for both species. As a result, both the dog and human body become sick. Dis-ease is directly associated with the mental condition that created it: separation anxiety, panic attack, split personality.

Think of it: *separation* anxiety, panic *attack*, and *split* personality all describe conflicts between two entities, ego and spirit, and two organisms, dogs and humans. Obviously, this is an unconscious process. I do not believe people intend to harm their animals, but the result is still problematic. People spend millions of dollars on behaviour modification when, in reality, money should go towards emotion modification. Star TV trainers lead viewers to believe they can change dog behaviour if they themselves exhibit dominant and aggressive behaviours. The leader of the pack training methods will not cure dogs; actually, the opposite occurs. Punishment will increase negative behaviour because it increases negative emotion. Hence, the old saying *anger begets more anger* is true. When projection occurs over long periods of time, corresponding biological problems arise.

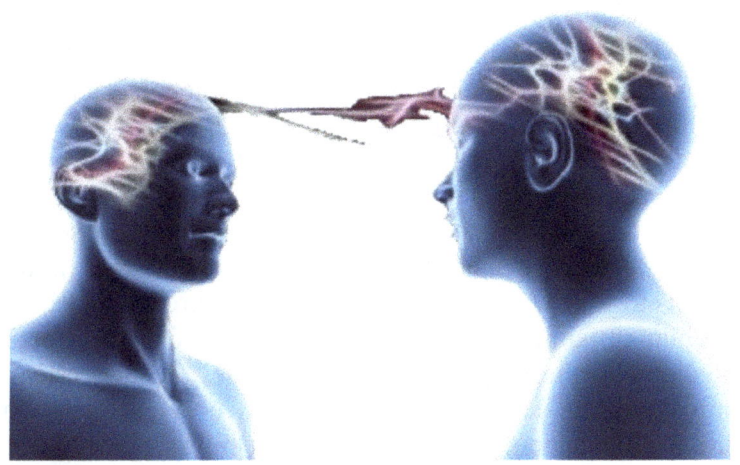

Figure 4. Electric currents exchange.

Case study: Scooby

Scooby is a good example of the genetic sociability theory. The male Rhodesian Ridgeback had lived in an outside large kennel with his siblings for his entire life. All the dogs were isolated from external stimuli. When I evaluated the dogs, Scooby was extremely well mannered and socially adjusted. This dog simply loved humans and other animals, but even well-adjusted dogs can, and do, exhibit anti-social behaviour.

A good example of this phenomenon involved four Rhodesian Ridgeback dogs I saw in consultation. A few years ago, a breeder in Mirabel asked me to evaluate a litter of adolescent dogs he was unable to place. Scooby, one of the four puppies, exhibited extreme fear and mildly aggressive responses towards people, and no one could approach him except the breeder himself. The three remaining dogs were fearful of humans. But the dogs began to approach me after several minutes of encouragement. My assessment revealed that three of the dogs displayed typical fear and flight responses toward normally harmless stimuli. However, I considered Scooby to be unpredictable and dangerous.

My conclusion: in all four cases, the socialization process had failed, not because of poor protocols or because something biological had gone wrong, except for Scooby. We decided to work very hard and trained the dogs to go towards strangers and bigger dogs. The clients refused medication and accepted the condition. Unfortunately, we could still see side effects. The breeder placed three adult dogs with strict training protocols to follow. The most curious of the three adjusted well to his human family, while the two others remained fearful and unpredictable throughout their lives. The breeder released Scooby, without fear of liability. I can only imagine what would have happened if these dogs had been Irish Wolfhounds.

While some behaviour problems link directly to social development because of improper exposure during the critical phase, other behaviour issues link to genetics. I hope that the discovery of a sociability gene, or combination of genes, will help animal professionals adequately assess behaviour, seek proper medication, and apply appropriate behaviour modification protocols. Scooby could have benefited from pharmaceutical support throughout his development and should have received proper training during socialization to give him the extra push he needed. The next case advances this reflection further.

Case study: Boreal

The next case illustrates how genetic social behaviour research can benefit professional animal behaviour consultants and trainers. When I first met Boreal (Figure 5), she was a ten-month-old, intact female Belgium Shepherd Groenendael, who had been actively chasing moving objects, from animate or inanimate, for the previous three months. Although she demonstrated great intelligence, her attention span required lots of work. Boreal spent the first eight months of her life in a crate at a dog grooming facility. The grooming facility owner constantly exposed her to high levels of stimuli and poor social contact. Strangely, her social skills towards humans and dogs were good, and she exhibited excellent behaviour towards unfamiliar dogs.

Boreal should have been the poster dog for fear or insecure aggression commonly associated with poor socialization. But it appeared that the overstimulating environment had succeeded in shaping her personality to the emotionally dispersed creature I now had in front of me. Unable to focus, she would be continually distracted by squirrels, birds, cats, bicycles, skateboards, floating objects, children, even her shadow. People described the dog as diffused. I agreed. The final behavioural assessment revealed that she was highly stressed and overwhelmingly troubled; yet there she was, happy as can be.

During her stay in the grooming facility, she could not exhibit normal dog behaviours such as barking, rough-play, or environmental investigation. Boreal did not receive appropriate levels of physical and cognitive exercise, yet she did not demonstrate anti-social behaviours. None of those issues troubled her adoptive human, for she took Boreal, knowing she would probably be a handful. Her only request was that I turn Boreal into her running companion. As my behaviour students often say, *Oy!* I knew this was going to be a challenge, and I was not wrong.

Our first behaviour consultation was in May of 2005. When I arrived, a frantically barking Boreal and her overwhelmed caregiver, Louise, greeted me. I stood there for a moment to let the dog investigate and then suggested we move into the kitchen area. We discussed the situation and the problems she was experiencing. Louise had two goals for Boreal: first, that I teach Boreal to heel so they could both enjoy a run, and second that I stop her from barking when people knocked on the door. Never would I have guessed, at that moment, that this over-excited and stressed out Boreal—aka "Miss Einstein"—would have changed my life. I even wrote about her in a French dog magazine called

Passionnément Chien because the world needed to know what I am about to tell you.

Figure 5. Photo of Boreal

After a few visits and a very unsuccessful power-walking session, I realized that Boreal needed to learn how to focus, and Louise needed to get her anxiety under control. The following week, I designed and proposed a social cognitive development program for Boreal and her human. The program I designed had two objectives: 1. train Boreal in object recognition and 2. teach Louise to acknowledge her emotions. My plan was to combine both objectives into one goal. I would teach Louise to work with Boreal while acknowledging her emotions as she trained. I would also teach her to recognize canine displacement behaviours, such as appeasement and avoidance signals.

The objective was to control Boreal's extroverted personality. This new training protocol would allow Louise to understand and establish a trusting relationship, which would concentrate Boreal's emotionally diffused energy onto one focal point. Both would learn to respect each other's boundaries and emotional threshold. All this would take place in the kitchen, the preferred environment. I introduced Boreal to clicker training and her career as canine savant took off after our first session. When I left that day, I had planned for Boreal to learn twelve objects. I told Louise that two objects each day would be enough. I did not want to exhaust Boreal and stress her more. That was on a Thursday. Louise called me on Saturday, sobbing. Boreal knew all 12 objects with an accuracy of ten on ten. *Oy!* turned to *Holy Cow!*

Within a few weeks, Boreal could discriminate between thirty-two different objects with an accuracy rate of one hundred percent. Unfortunately, she understood the nature of the game and soon became bored. We increased the challenge and introduced words on laminated cards, such as "tricycle" and "Pony" The objective was to teach her word-object recognition. We were both certain this would take a while. To Louise's utter disbelief, Boreal mastered this task in two weeks. I remember the phone call as if it were yesterday. The panicked voice on the other end of the phone said: "*She learned eighteen words today. I only have a few more left until our next meeting! What am I going to do? This dog is incredible!*" I laughed and then went to work.

During the following training session, I decided to try to teach Boreal to read. We taught her the touch and take actions. "Touch" meant nose to object; "take" meant pickup with mouth and drop. The following objective was to associate the word on the card with the action touch or take. Little Miss Einstein—her new nickname by then—took her job very seriously and learned with enthusiasm. I associated the object, name card, actions, and action card together. In other words, I would show her the touch or take verb card followed by an object name card and she would perform the required task.

When Boreal saw the touch bunny card, she would look at her objects and touch her bunny. We mixed all the words together, yet she rarely failed. If we tried to dupe her by not placing the object, she would go to her workbox and look in it. She was one smart cookie. Within a few weeks, Louise and Boreal had a success rate of ninety percent. As the cognitive program grew in complexity, so did their relationship. Boreal had started to exhibit aggression towards anyone, other than Louise or me, who would approach her *workbox*.[4]

One day, I received the dreaded phone call: Boreal had bitten a child Louise had previously treated in her osteopathy home office. I did a little investigation and discovered that Boreal had previously exhibited anxiety when introduced to this particular child. The day she bit him, the child was moving towards the training box Boreal so eagerly protected. In Boreal's disapproving dog mind, she had no other option than to take the matter into her own mouth.

From then on, a decision was made, I would teach Boreal and Louise how to identify and effectively manage their emotions. Louise found it increasingly difficult to control her anxiety and this confused Boreal. The training routine was arduous to keep up and frustrated both parties. As a result of our mixed messages, Boreal became impatient; the message she interpreted from her human caregiver was Stay calm, but hurry up while you do! A few weeks later, I decided to change the training routine, and Boreal became a model student.

The first few sessions were done at my home. Boreal would come to my house, and we would work on her problem-solving abilities and physical discomfort. Boreal was a stressed dog, so I would start our training sessions with a massage. Boreal would go through the same exercises, but this time, she would work with me. Since my emotional connection to Boreal was very different from Louise, things worked out very well.

Boreal would diligently sit or lie in front of me and wait for commands. If she did not work fast enough, Boreal would look at me, stand, and pace. My goal was to teach her to be patient and redirect her attention to the task. My hope was that Boreal would focus her remarkable abilities towards one focal point, herself. I taught Louise how to teach Boreal to take ownership of her emotions. As a result, something amazing happened: Louise learned to do the same.

---

[4] Louise would place Boreal's thirty-two objects, on the laminated cards, and the math cubes in a special box in her office.

The connection that Louise, Boreal and I shared was remarkable. The connection allowed us to progress at an amazing pace and achieve our cognitive, emotional, and environmental goals in no time. We only experienced a few minor emotional setbacks that directly correlated to human issues. When Louise would call to tell me that Boreal was acting out, I would ask what had changed in her personal or professional life recently. From then on, Louise started to identify her dog's reactions as a reflection of her own emotional state. Louise could then change her reactions in order to correct Boreal's behaviour. One could say Boreal became her personal projection therapist.

As it turned out, Boreal became a wonderful teacher as well as a dearly loved student. Although the beginning of her life was inadequate, something in Boreal refused to surrender. I like to believe that she inherited an awesome set of genes. Before you ask, I have met five possible "Einstein" dogs in my career so far. Unfortunately, the human component of the team has always been unwilling to push their dog's abilities. Since a training session for an Einstein dog can last nearly two hours, that might explain why people do not want to commit to such a rigorous training protocol.

Case study: Stick

The next case involved a two-year-old, neutered male Dachshund named Stick and an insecure woman named Linda. Our first consultation took place in September 2005. The functional behaviour assessment (FBA) revealed a high predatory instinct, people and dog-directed aggression, insecurity, and a low trainability score. Linda, a single woman in her forties, worked as a legal secretary, who was absent from home from nine to five. When we first met, Stick demonstrated aggressive behaviours and continuously barked at me. Linda was concerned about his recent attacks on cats but was uncertain what to do about it. The owner acquired Stick from a reputable breeder at the tender age of seven weeks, and the dog had been neutered at eleven months. He started exhibiting behaviour issues at the tender age of only two months.

By February 2004, Stick had seriously wounded the cat, bitten two adults and attacked a child. Although well socialized with dogs and people during the critical period, Stick was not a social dog. He preferred to stay close to his human and rarely interacted with other dogs. When dogs came too close, Stick would lunge and chase them away. In contrast to Boreal, Stick should have been the poster dog of social behaviour because of a successful socialization period. He was not. During our initial visit, Linda confessed she had interpersonal issues and jokingly mentioned her dog was suffering from the same problem. She was closer to the truth than she realized. Linda and I discussed her situation over a warm cup of herbal tea.

My goal was to gather as much information as possible in order to assess the human-dog relationship and set them up for success.[5] I wanted to experiment with social cognitive training plans. Linda said she was OK with this idea, so we started our journey the following week.

Had I been tactless enough to say that I thought Stick's behaviour was a direct result of Linda's emotional state, it would have further disrupted their relationship, and indirectly increased the dog's aggressive behaviour. In my experience, the best strategy for dealing with emotions is to slowly introduce them into one's consciousness is. People often become aggressive or emotionally detached when they perceive an attack from someone or perceive negative situations or potential conflicts.

Remember the example of the battery connection (+/-) (-/+) that creates disturbances? In order to overcome this potential problem, Linda needed to develop a trusting relationship with Stick. She also needed to trust her abilities as

---

[5] Placing a person, or dog, in a situation where every variable, frequency, duration, environment, and participant, is controlled by the counsellor/consultant. The intended objective of conditioning and social learning is to insure success.

a human leader[6] and animal caregiver. Again, the social-cognitive theory was the key concept in this case because I did not want to increase mistrust in either Linda or Stick. The positive results I anticipated would strengthen their relationship, not jeopardize it.

Behaviour outcome

Behaviour is the result of a response to an inner or outer stimulus. The organism classifies the outcome as positive or negative. There is no way around it; the stimulus directly links the positive or negative outcome. The new physical, mental or emotional response is then stored in the memory for future reference. Positive outcomes often take longer to achieve than negative ones. The reason is survival. If the dog approaches an ember and burns his nose, the nervous system sends a message: WARNING! FIRE BURNS. Thus, fire has the ability to end life. Negative outcomes = avoidance.

Conversely, if the dog eats a rat, the nervous system also sends a message: WARNING! EATING RATS TASTE OK . . . I GUESS. The rat might not taste too good, but the belly got full; thus, the rat-eating behaviour will increase, over time. Positive outcomes = increase. Thus, new behaviours take longer to learn when compared to negative behaviours. Why? you ask. Because to survive means to avoid death, but it also means trying new things. I wrote the positive message in a smaller font to remind you visually of the following: dogs go through life trying to avoid unpleasant consequences and increase pleasant ones.

From a social cognitive point of view, a dysfunctional relationship between a human and dog develops from unresolved past emotions, negative outcomes, and an adverse environment. The question now is what do dysfunctional

---

[6] Leader or leadership refers to the ability to guide a subject towards a predetermined goal without the use of verbal or physical force.

relationships look like. In a dysfunctional relationship, animals often fall victim to emotional projection because they themselves do not exhibit defence mechanisms. Because dogs are incapable of projecting their emotions, as such, they are defenceless in the hands of troubled human egos. Thankfully, nature has provided animals with a wonderful ability; dogs live in the eternal moment.

Canines live in the here-and-now with moderate to little emphasis on past or future experiences to influence their choices. Every event is a new experience in which emotions are relatively short-lived. Dogs exist synchronously with the environment in a state of quasi perpetual satisfaction and contentment, as long as their social, cognitive, and biological needs are satisfied. Darkness, so to speak, does not exist, and joy is all that dogs experience. The light immerses the self in a peaceful and soothing energy that the dog has come to emulate. Pet caregivers understand this concept, can grasp their dog's unique ability and fully share their joy.

We have seen how thoughts of separation lead to emotional projection, and that same emotional projection creates an energy discrepancy. For the average pet owner, this definition remains abstract. Concretely, projection occurs when emotions are no longer within a functional threshold range. At this point, the person seeks an outlet and triggers the defence mechanism. As we discussed, the emotional discharge process in people helps liberate tensions associated with feelings of emptiness, anger, frustration, or fear. In animals, the projection process would be relatively similar.

However, the unconscious belief in separation is impossible for animals. The dog mind does not live in the past or future; consequently, canines do not believe in separation because they cannot conceptualize the idea in the space-time continuum.[7] Furthermore, the present moment, by definition, implies that dogs assess situations based on experience, in order to predict a possible future outcome. Dogs can apply past

---

[7] Space-time continuum is defined as a single continuous movement through space and time.

information to present events; we call that process of storing information, memory. However, the ability to predict a future outcome, which is most likely very different for dogs, makes emotional projection highly unlikely.

Here is an example. My dog Albear wants to jump up on the couch because he remembers that my son Olivier let him do it three days ago at his house. Albear also remembers that Olivier sort of grinned before he accepted the request. Albear now replicates the same behaviour. But I refuse and point him to his own bed. Now, if Albear had the ability to predict a possible future outcome, he should have hidden his bed, torn the bed to shreds, peed on it, buried it in the yard, etc. The list could go on because the particular fate of the bed in future holds endless possibilities, and Albear would have planned for at least one of them.

Another example is jealousy. To be jealous, one has to remember an experience of losing a loved one to someone else, apply the memory to a present situation with a new partner, and expect the same outcome in the future. To prevent the past from repeating itself, people become very controlling of other people. Thankfully, dogs do not have it in them.

What dogs do have is fifteen thousand years of evolution and domestication. In fact, the emergence of *Canis familiaris* as a separate species is a direct consequence of their human social attraction. When people started to breed and care for these new dogs, they had no idea this intervention would spawn the emergence of a symbiotic partnership. A relationship in which humans turn to domestic dogs for specific services and dogs turned to humans for their survival. Regrettably, our symbiotic relationship can, and does, generate behaviour problems previously unheard of in the canine ethogram.

Today we have science and tools to reverse the process. We can change undesirable into desirable behaviour. Human and dog relationships based on negative emotional charges can benefit from the mirroring technique. With little more than an imaginary mirror, you can stop the projection and heal the perception. Let me explain how you can accomplish this Herculean task.

Reader notes

Chapter 4: Modifying Behaviour

Behaviour modification rules

When we discuss human behaviour modification techniques, people generally refer to the process as therapy or psychotherapy. When we discuss animal problems, behaviour modification remains the appropriate term to use. As such, behaviour modification is the process by which an undesirable behaviour, or negative action, is transformed into a desirable behaviour, or positive action (Chance, 2008). The modification process never eliminates, cures, or fixes the negative behaviour.

Behaviour modification only strives to change or transform undesirable behaviour into a new positive outcome, action, or reaction. In highly stressful situations, the former undesirable behaviour will prevail, for the involuntary response to a stimulus has become a reflex (Chance, 2008). To change an unconditioned impulse or a conditioned into a *new* conditioned response is extremely long and complex. Fortunately, tools exist which can make the behaviour modification process a little faster and easier. We can also change conditioned emotional responses into new behaviour with classical and operant conditioning.

Dog behaviour modification and training might seem unrealistic for many people, yet certain individuals constantly train whether they know or not. Here is how it occurs. The average dog needs approximately fifteen repetitive associations between two stimuli or events to learn the connection between the two. A good example of training without knowing is the association your dog has made between your shoes, jacket, wallet or purse, and car keys and you're leaving the house. You did not purposefully train the *leave home* behaviour with rewards; nonetheless, dogs learn that the particular sequence of behaviours means you are going away without them.

Now, change a behaviour, say, take the leash instead of wallet/purse, and dogs know they are coming with you. The attachment we share with our dogs allows them to make associations between social cues and consequences. Left gaze bias, the process by which we visually read emotions on a person's face by scanning from left to right takes on a new meaning when we look at it from an animal training point of view.

Before we move on, here is a little exercise designed to help you understand how behaviour modification works. As fast as you can, interlace your fingers together and keep them in this position for thirty seconds. Now, consciously change the position of your fingers: lace them in the opposite direction. See the following image for guidance (Figure 6). This new position might feel strange and somewhat uncomfortable, but if you keep practicing the new behaviour, it will eventually feel comfortable.

Imagine you practiced the new finger position behaviour for six months and on the seventh month, I asked you to stretch your arms out by your side, hold the extended arm position for thirty seconds and on the count of three, I told you to interlace your fingers as fast as possible. Unquestionably, you would use the same familiar finger position you started with, because the behaviour is an unconscious response, and no amount of conditioning can override the finger lacing action once it imprints on the brain and becomes a reflex. As Chance (2008) so clearly stated: "A reflex is a *relationship* between certain kinds of events, usually events in the immediate surroundings, and certain kinds of behaviours." (p.9)

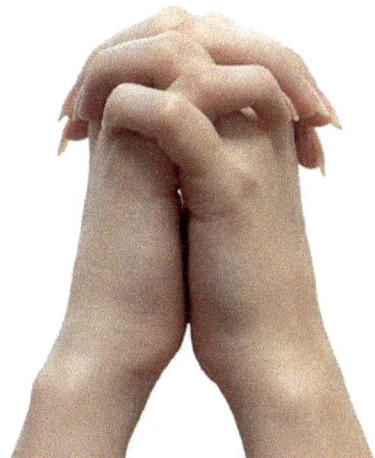

Figure 6. Interlaced fingers left-right and right-left.

Behaviour modification protocols

Temperament and character constitute an individual. Temperament is the sum of all the genetic traits an animal is born with. These traits are not modifiable. Character, on the other hand, is extremely modifiable because it equals the sum of all life experiences. If a dog is born an eight-out-of-ten[8] on the fear continuum, no amount of conditioning will reduce it to zero. If the dog learned to be fearful because of experiences, or lack thereof, conditioning would help modify the behaviour by a few score points in either direction: higher or lower.

Thus, behaviour modification focuses on changing character, not temperament. A behaviour modification protocol attempts to create new positive associations in order to change character. Specialists created a series of protocols to help animals. When we follow accurate steps at very specific times, we obtain similar results. Behaviour modification protocols are like psychological recipes, so to speak. The most commonly used protocols are systematic desensitization, counter conditioning, habituation, and flooding.

---

[8] On a scale of one to ten, ten being the worst.

Systematic desensitization is a behaviour modification protocol we use to change an undesirable behaviour into a desirable one through a series of small successive approximations. The process is designed to gradually expose the dog to the stimulus that elicits the behaviour, yet keeps it under stimulus control. We keep dogs under their emotional threshold to increase the likelihood a positive outcome will occur each time. Trainers give reinforcement after the dog exhibits the desirable behaviour. The dog receives reinforcement for the desired behaviour as we either ignore or stop undesirable behaviour.

The most effective way to utilize systematic desensitization is to place the dog in a situation that will elicit a response but not trigger a reaction. Here is an example: your dog Rex reacts to other dogs at a distance of 20ft (6.1 m); we expose Rex to an aggressive dog situation 15ft (4.6 m) away to avoid a reaction. A decoy dog will approach, and Rex will receive reinforcement in the form of a food treat if, and only if, he does not react. The desirable behaviour might be to sit calmly and silently. The distance at which Rex reacts is critical because it must not trigger the undesirable behaviour.

The new *when-you-see-another-dog,-sit-stay-and-remain-calm* behaviour will eventually replace the old *when-you-see-a-dog,-jump,-bark,-pull,-and-get-all-excited* behaviour. Systematic desensitization is all about working in baby steps. In trainer lingo, we call it *setting the dog up for success*. As Richard Dreyfuss explains to Bill Murray in the movie *What About Bob* (1991), "Baby steps. It means setting small reasonable goals for yourself one day at a time, one tiny step at a time."

Counter conditioning is another popular behaviour modification protocol that rewards a desirable behaviour incompatible with an undesirable behaviour. Jumping on people is a good example. Imagine Rex jumps on people and you want the behaviour to stop. In counter conditioning, you would reinforce Rex when all his four feet are on the floor instead of on family members, counters, or tables. When used competently, this simple recipe can have a dramatic effect on Rex and your canine companion relationship.

In a few simple repetitions, dogs can learn new behaviours at a very high rate of performance. However, if we do not apply counter conditioning properly, it can reinforce the old behaviour and set Rex up for failure. One of my favourite counter conditioning behaviours is silence. I think people misconstrue silence as a behaviour, and never think to reinforce it. As the Rush song "Freewill" goes, "If you choose not to decide, you still have made a choice." So why not choose to reward the silent choice; after all, it is incompatible with barking, is it not?

Habituation occurs when an undesirable behaviour decreases over time. This behaviour modification protocol does not involve classical or operant conditioning. By definition, habituation is a non-associative learning process; as such, it should not be confused with extinction, which is the gradual elimination of a conditioned response. During a behaviour modification session, we expose the dog to the stimulus that elicits the undesirable behaviour at random or fixed intervals until the desirable behaviour increases. Normally, habituation involves the reduction of a naturally occurring biological or psychological response (Chance, 2008). The dog does not receive reinforcement or punishment during the process. The objective is to get the animal habituated to a stimulus.

Habituation protocols do not strive to teach an alternate desirable behaviour and are sometimes confused with flooding. The two protocols may seem similar to the uninitiated. Therefore, I will use the same example to describe both protocols. This time, our undesirable behaviour will be fear of doorbells. In habituation, Rex hears the pre-recorded sound of the doorbell and runs to hide under the bed. The trainer takes Rex back to the living room and the owners ring the doorbell again.

The professional repeats the process many times in the same training session to get the dog habituated to the loud sound. Some people might increase the sound of the doorbell over time; however, in true habituation, the sound is at a predetermined intensity. Once the dog habituates to the sound and no longer reacts fearfully when he hears the doorbell, the protocol is over. The dog never receives reinforcement or punishment during the process.

Professional trainers must make sure true habituation has occurred and that the non-response is not due to sensory adaption or motor fatigue. Sensory adaptation occurs when transduction[9] has stopped and perception no longer takes place. Motor fatigue occurs when the sensory organ still perceives, but the body can no longer react. Unfortunately, uneducated trainers can harm dogs when they use protocols they do not understand, and, as you have just read, habituation is a complex approach to changing an unpleasant behaviour into a desirable one. This was a brief description of an elaborate process meant to increase your knowledge of behaviour modification protocols. We will not spend much time on these, as we have much to cover in the following chapters. I would strongly recommend you hire a science-based trainer to help you address your dog-related problems, should you wish to embark on the habituation methodology.

The behaviour modification protocol called flooding occurs when dog trainers expose dogs to a stimulus that elicits the undesirable behaviour until the undesirable response is no longer present. Technically, there is no limit on time: flooding sessions last the amount of time the process takes for the behaviour to diminish. In flooding, there is no reinforcement because the absence of response is the new desired behaviour (Chance, 2008). The dog seems cured once the flooding protocol is over.

However, the use of classical conditioning without proper knowledge can have adverse effects. A well-documented negative outcome of flooding techniques results in learned helplessness. Inhibition and learned helplessness might appear similar on the surface because dogs appear to have been cured. But in reality, they can no longer respond emotionally or

---

9 The process of converting sound, light, odours and sensation into cognitive information through the sensory organs.

cognitively when they have learned to no longer display stress, fear, or anxiety behaviours. With time, learned helplessness can lead to depression. Inhibition, on the other hand, is an impulse control strategy. Inhibited dogs do not display species-specific behaviours when faced with stimuli that normally elicit responses. Back to our example. In flooding, a trainer exposes the dog to the maximum sound intensity of the doorbell until he no longer reacts to it, regardless of the time it takes.

We have looked at classical and operant conditioning, but to grasp the complexities of behaviourism, one must understand the guiding principles used in behaviour modification. In operant conditioning, animals strive to gain something, such as reinforcement, or avoid something, such as punishment. In turn, reinforcement and punishment are either positive or negative. To summarize: both reinforcement and punishment can be either positive or negative. We write these quadrants (Figure 7) as positive reinforcement, negative reinforcement, positive punishment, and negative punishment.

Rex sit (↑ behaviour) + cookie (reinforcement) = R+

Rex sit (↑ behaviour) − social pressure (reinforcement) = R−

Rex sit (↓ behaviour) + slap on nose (punishment) = P+

Rex sit (↓ behaviour) − cookie (punishment) = P−

You may well be wondering how punishment can be positive and how reinforcement can be negative. And you are not alone. Positive reinforcement (R+) increases the probability a given behaviour will occur again because the dog received something he wanted, such as food, toys, or affection. Negative reinforcement (R−) increases the probability a given behaviour will occur again because the dog experienced something he did not want, such as discomfort, pain, or social pressure. Positive punishment (P+) reduces the probability a given behaviour will occur again, because the dog received something unpleasant, such as a choke, electric shock, punch, or kick. Finally, negative punishment (P-) reduces the probability a given behaviour will occur again because the dog

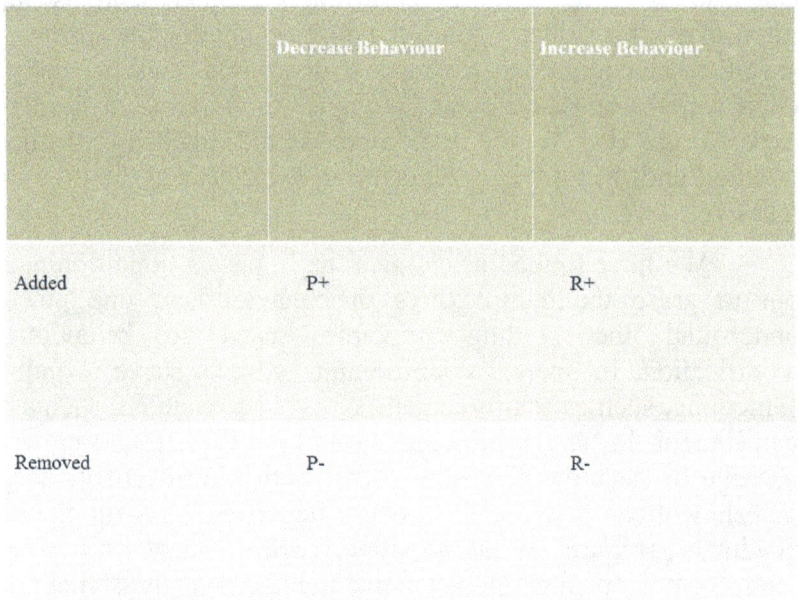

Figure 7. Operant conditioning quadrants.

did not receive something he wanted, such as food, toy, or affection.

Following are a few examples of each quadrant using the *sit* behaviour. The behaviour arrow indicates what we want in terms of a result. The arrow pointing up means I want the behaviour to occur again, and the arrow pointing down means I want the behaviour to go away. Reinforcement means I am giving something to the dog and punishment means I am taking something away from the dog.

When we use operant conditioning, we use all of the quadrants to shape behaviour towards our intended goal. We are like mind engineers who play with the brain to change behaviour, normally for the better. We can push training further if we add a few elements to the conditioning process. Professional trainers can add a continuous schedule of reinforcement, such as variables or fixed intervals and ratios of reinforcement. It all depends on the desired objective and the particular dog. Each combination of these five schedules serves to create or maintain a behaviour once it is learned.

Here are some definitions which will help you better understand the case studies presented in later chapters. We use continuous schedules of reinforcement (CSRs) during the acquisition phase of behaviour. With CSRs, every performance of the behaviour will result in reinforcement.

- *Fixed-ratio schedules* will yield reinforcement after a specific number of responses or after the dog offers a fixed number of behaviours: sit five times, and you will get a treat. This schedule will keep dogs moderately motivated to learn.
- *Variable-ratio schedules* result in reinforcement after an unpredictable number of responses, or after we ask the dog for variable number of behaviours. This schedule will keep dogs highly motivated.
- *Fixed-interval schedules* will offer reinforcement after a specific amount of time has passed, or when the dog performs the behaviour after a fixed period has passed, say five minutes. This schedule of reinforcement will result in a low motivation rate.
- *Variable-interval schedules* will yield reinforcement after an unpredictable lapse of time, or when the dog performs the behaviour after variable periods of time, for example, every five, three, one, four, and five minutes have passed between behaviours. This schedule results in a very slow motivation rate.

Combining the proper behaviour modification protocol with the appropriate learning theory produces alterations in behaviour. A professional animal behaviour specialist or trainer teaches pet caregivers how to combine and use these techniques. Should the process fail, the culprit is most likely miscommunication or a lack of experience or knowledge. Remember, the source of the conflict in the troubled relationship does not come from the dog; it is simply an outward projection which originates from the human mind. Many pet owners become highly stressed, anxious, or emotionally perturbed to see dog behaviour evolve negatively. Consequently, it is counterproductive—not to mention unethical and rude—to overtly tell a client that their dog's undesirable behaviour is a direct result of their own emotional state.

On the other hand, pet caregivers should recognize the source of their emotional problems in order to counter their dogs' reactions. Mirroring helps to identify the source of the behaviour problem and its consequences for the human-dog relationship. This understanding paves the way to effective problem-solving strategies. Remember that dogs can and do read human emotions via the left-gaze bias (LGB) I described earlier (Guo et al., 2009). In biology 101, we learn that the left hemisphere controls the right side of the body and vice versa; therefore, when the brain scans the left side of the face controlled by the emotional right side of the brain, dogs notice our emotions and adjust their behaviour accordingly.

Armed with our knowledge of behaviour learning theory, LGB, and projection, we begin to see how dogs know much more about us than we previously thought. However, we can change the outcome of situations by adjusting our behaviour and teaching the dog a new alternate response. Look at the images in Figure 8. Photo 2 is the right side of my face copied and flipped. Photo 3 is the left side of my face copied and flipped. Which face appears happier? If you said photo 3, you are experiencing left gaze bias. Just as with the following picture of my dog Albear (chapter 7), our face displays subtle emotional differences between the left and right side of the face. The effect is difficult to observe without this trickery, but our brains have learned to make this distinction, which allows for a more accurate emotional assessment.

When presented with pictures of human faces, monkeys, canines, or inanimate objects, our furry companions demonstrate the left gaze bias only towards human faces (Guo et al., 2009). In terms of behaviour modification and training, the left gaze bias proves that dogs can, indeed, read human emotions, allowing pet caregivers to use this information to identify emotional states and train new behaviours.

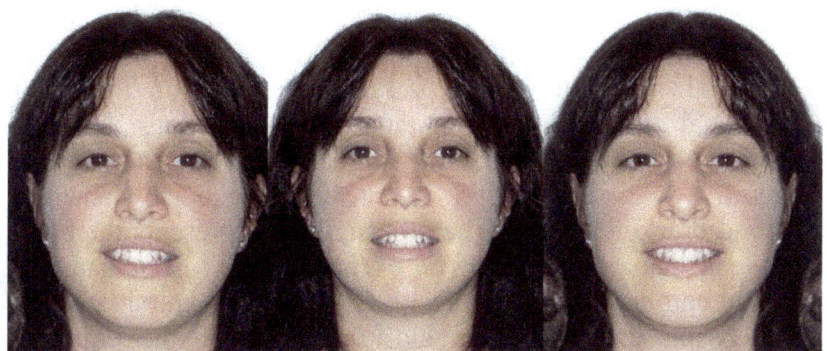

Figure 8. Left-gaze bias: Gaby.

The convergence point

The convergence of universal energy theories, emotional projection, learning theories, behaviour modification protocols, concepts of attachment, and the mirroring process might confuse many readers, but they are actually relatively easy to understand. To help you work through this challenge, think of the battery connection mentioned earlier. We align batteries in a specific sequence in order for them to produce power. If you do not align the batteries in the proper order, the battery cannot function.

Similarly, if you do not align with your dog, you will have a dysfunctional relationship. To understand how human-dog relationships work; I designed a battery analogy to explain traditional relationships. The symbol for a dysfunctional relationship is Ø, and for a functional relationship O. Relationships between two living beings resemble the battery pattern in electronic equipment and generate four possible patterns represented as:

- pattern one [-/+ -/+] + [-/+ -/+] = O
- pattern two [-/+ +/-] + [-/+ +/-] = Ø
- pattern three [+/- -/+] + [+/- -/+] = Ø
- pattern four [+/- +/-] + [+/- +/-] = Ø

The symbol (-/+) represents the direction in which emotional energy flows between humans and dogs. Imagine the line of a circle connected at both ends to create a complete circuit. The first bracket [ ] represents the human and the second bracket the dog. The plus sign (+) represents the bond between human and dog. The exchange between human and animal can be positive or negative, but rarely neutral between two living entities. That said, the parts of the equation represented by the brackets are what interest us because that is where behaviour problems arise.

In pattern number one, both human and dog share a comfortable reciprocal exchange. The circular formula would simply create a positive exchange. In a reciprocal exchange, emotional projection is absent. Humans intuitively recognize that their own emotions do not belong to dogs. The positive emotional connection flows outwardly from one person, passes through the dog, and back, without any negativity. It is beautiful to watch.

Two organisms symbiotically linked together through empathetic species-specific unconscious emotional ties. A dog shares its life with a human, as a dog; a human shares its life with a dog, as a human. The perfect symbiotic partnership is an inter-species morphic field in the making.

When projection does occur, however, one can work on awareness to stop the projection and reclaim a functional relationship, and I will tell you how to do just that in the upcoming chapters. On our way there, please keep an open mind. This chapter is not about criticizing you or your current situation. No one can fully be mindful all the of time and avoid projection one hundred percent. Every human has told another human to *buzz off*. The same goes for dogs.

Problems occur when we do it over, and over, and over again and do nothing to repair damaged relationships. A negatively charged positive human means an egoless person charged with negative emotions, and a positively charged negative person means an ego charged with positive emotions. The same applies to dogs. This implies dogs have an ego as per the definition of ego as a conscious thinking subject.

Pattern one: [-/+ -/+] : negatively charged positive human does not project positivity
+ : onto
[-/+ -/+] : negatively charged positive dog does not receive positive projection
= O: functional relationship (+/+ no projection)

Pattern two: [-/+ +/-] : negatively charged positive human projects negativity
+ : onto
[-/+ +/-] : negatively charged positive dog receives negative projection
= Ø : dysfunctional relationship (+/- projection)

Pattern three: [+/- -/+]: positively charged negative human does not project positivity
+: onto
[+/- -/+]: positively charged negative dog does not receive positive projection
= Ø: dysfunctional relationship (-/+ projection)

Pattern four: [+/- +/-]: positively charged negative human project negativity
+: onto
[+/- +/-]: positively charged negative dog receives negative projection.
= Ø: dysfunctional relationship (-/- projection)

Patterns two, three and four cause behaviour problems because they disrupt the energy flow and project outward in the form of emotional disturbances. The middle of the bracket demonstrates the direction of the projection; consequently, you can read the following formula for the above dysfunctional pattern, number four, as [+/- +/-] + [+/- +/-] = Ø. Bear in mind, however, that the formulas serve to explain a circular form, not a linear one. The current comes back to the human once it leaves the dog and the cycle is completed.

Behaviour problems do not occur within single projection cycles. Behaviour problems arise when cycles repeat themselves on the space-time continuum. In the previous formulas, you saw the outcome of the projection, as in: human gets/dog loses, human loses/dog gets, and human loses/dog loses. The functional relationship would read: human gets/dog gets, a typical win/win outcome, hence the symbiotic relationship model. Simple, no? Deviant behaviour is the result of emotional projection, but it is not a proverbial death sentence. We do have ways to re-establish functional behaviours between humans and dogs. The mirror technique is one of them.

Mirroring is the conscious psychological action that serves to momentarily stop the projection and establish a new positive energy flow through the (+/+) convention. Imagine if you placed a mirror between two batteries to stop the flow of energy. No need to overthink, it would look something like this [-/+ +/-] ▯ [-/+ +/-]. In our projection formula patterns, the mirror replaces the plus onto sign (+: onto). The mirror helps the person to stop projecting and redirects the energy flow towards its original source: you and me.

The psychological procedure serves as a momentary barrier between two individuals in conflict. The momentary pause allows each person to observe their projection, stop the process, and reclaim the deviant behaviour as their own. In this way, individuals take ownership of their emotional state, make the proper mental and emotional adjustments, modify their actions and behaviours accordingly, and proceed with the exchange without projecting their distorted beliefs onto others. In *A Course in Miracles* (2007) we read, "The ultimate purpose of projection, as the ego uses it, is always to get rid of guilt." (ACIM, T-13.II.1:1). When projection throws fuel on the fire, mirroring puts it out.

> *The inappropriate use of extension, or projection, occurs when you believe that some emptiness or lack exists in you and that you can fill it with your own ideas instead of the truth.* (ACIM, 2007, T-2.I.1:7)

Reader notes

Chapter 5: Unity

The mirroring process

Emotional projection is not a new psychological phenomenon. Freud described projection as a psychological defence mechanism (Freud, 1937). Psychologists group defence mechanisms into four levels: immature, mature, neurotic, and pathological. Defence mechanisms help people cope with a variety of emotional strains, ranging from simple life-related issues to long-lasting trauma. Each level divides into groups according to age, intensity, and duration of coping strategy (Schacter et al., 2015).

We can describe the short-term coping strategy as either a complex immature process or the creation of a long-term management strategy that develops into defence mechanisms in adolescents and young adults; these are characterized by acting out, fantasy, idealization, passive aggression, projection, projective identification, and somatization.

These psychological strategies normally do not last very long. On the one hand, mature adults tend to use simple short-term coping defence mechanisms, such as altruism, anticipation, humour, identification, introjection, sublimation, and thought suppression. Although these mechanisms are less severe, they serve to minimize or avoid emotional disturbances. Neurotic adults, on the other, tend to use more complex short-term coping defence mechanisms, such as displacement, dissociation, hypochondriasis, isolation, intellectualization, rationalization, reaction formation, regression, repression, undoing, and withdrawal. Pathological adult complex long-term coping or psychotic defence mechanisms are characterized by delusional projection, denial, distortion, and splitting (Freud, 1937; Hughes & Riordan, 2017).

Mirroring refers to the process by which an individual unconsciously imitates another. Mirror neurons seem to be responsible for the process behind this form of unconscious, emotional imitation (Rizzolatti & Craighero, 2004; Rizzolatti, 2005; Rizzolatti, & Fabbri-Destro, 2008). The fundamental objective of mirroring is to recognize conflict as one unconscious emotional event united by similar imitational responses. In our human-dog interactions, we consciously observe the emotional relationship in order to identify and change our reactions.

My goal is to modify dog behaviour through mirroring. In human-human relationships, Peter projects his unconscious thoughts onto Marie, and subsequently perceives an attack; Marie, however, feels attacked and defends herself through another defence mechanism such as denial, which reinforces person Peter's projection. Conflict is simply a misleading perception based on false thoughts and beliefs.

In other words, the individual experiencing the emotional response sees in someone else what is occurring in his own subconscious and imitates the behaviour. Imagine that you and I are arguing through a glass window. I believe you are the source of my negative experiences and feelings, and you believe I am responsible for your negative experience, so the argument match begins. Unfortunately, this type of emotional battle normally ends with one perceived victor.

Mirroring places a metaphorical two-sided mirror between persons Peter and Marie. By doing so, individuals rapidly realize they can only argue with themselves. Consequently, people take responsibility for their emotional reactions, thoughts and ideas, and the conflict ends, because the direction of the emotional energy flow was changed. After all, "Projection makes perception." (ACIM, T-21.In.1:1).

Recognizing conflict

When people experience conflict, they often fail to recognize their thoughts, ideas, and emotions as their own. People believe others are responsible for the terrible events occurring in their lives at that moment. When individuals argue, they may believe deeply that the other person (or group) is the cause of their negative emotions. However, in order to change the outcome of a conflict, people need to acknowledge that others, whether people or dogs, are not the source of their physical, mental, and emotional troubles. We term the ability to make such choices free will. Remember, conflict is motivated by fear, and fear originates from the unconscious belief that separation is real.

When you think you can lose something, the desire to fight for it overwhelms you, without your conscious awareness. Thanks to ego, we sometimes unconsciously bury free will in loud noise, visual or auditory stimuli, and negative thoughts. Rest assured we all have free will, for it is a fundamental element of what Walsch refers to as *Essential Essence* (2017), aka universal energy.

Another quote from *A Course in Miracles* (Shucman, 2007) summarizes the idea that the ego wants to see you in conflict, "Believing you are no longer you, you do not realize that you are failing yourself." (T-13.II.2:6). When people experience fearful events or conflicting situations, they often think they have only two choices: to perceive the situation as negative (fear) or positive (love). The ability to choose and make decisions based on either fear or love extends beyond the human species to include animals, more specifically, the domestic dog. Pet caregivers who develop awareness through insightful relationships and secure attachments can directly modify their pet's behaviour through desire and free will alone. In this way, individuals can use the mirror technique to identify and correct animal behaviour problems before they develop.

Concretely, you can accomplish a mirroring session in a few simple steps. I will guide you through the process, but first, you must recall a past conflict in order to analyze the situation. As you think of the most recent event, try to remain objective while completing the following statements. We will stir up emotions, so do not be too hard on yourself; yourSelf will benefit from our exploration. Step 1 simply serves to name the event you chose, should you want to return to this passage later on. You can even date the event for future reference.

Recognize the projection:
_____
_____
_____

- Place an imaginary mirror between you and the dog.
- Take three deep breaths.

Identify the negative emotion/s:
_____
_____
_____

- Remember, the dog has nothing to do with your reactions.

Select and apply a new reaction to the situation:
_____
_____
_____

Leave situation when change is impossible:
_____
_____
_____

- Do not dwell on your thoughts if you become overwhelmed.

The wonderful thing about emotional projection and the mirror technique is that once a person recognizes the projection, three-quarters of the work is done. Unfortunately, the process is not without its dichotomy: simplicity and complexity. Once you trigger an emotion, it becomes extremely difficult to disengage mentally. It is even more difficult when you are facing a person because the act of physically stepping away from the situation can increase anger. Social bonds tend to keep people in conflict, even though they know they should have walked away (Donatelle & Thompson, 2011). Martin Lawrence gave us the famous *talk to the hand 'cause the face don't give a damn,* which became popular in the early 90s. Although the phrase really meant *shut up, I don't want to hear about it*, it allowed people to simply walk away from conflict. It was a useful tool.

The wonderful thing about mirroring is that it applies to our human-dog relationships, too. Since people can experience distressing emotions at any given moment, individuals can conduct mirroring sessions with their pooch through simple dog behaviour observations. Pet caregivers can safely, and silently, establish a mirroring session to address their own misconduct or dog behaviour issues, anywhere and at any time. In the following case study, the client was able to apply the mirror technique and change the outcome of an evolving behaviour problem.

Case study: Jake

Sue acquired Jake, a 3-year-old sterilized, male Jack Russell, when he was a puppy. Jake is a high-energy dog that is always ready for action. Sue is a calm, peaceful, and relaxed yoga teacher. Although she loves the outdoors, Sue prefers the warmth and comfort of her studio apartment. Their human-animal relationship was normally peaceful, but several complications arose when she decided to move. Her main concern was Jake's almost obsessive-compulsive destructive behaviour. His desire to constantly empty cupboards, the clothes basket, the toy basket, and her moving boxes exhausted and annoyed Sue. She complained about the troublesome canine's rowdiness, his lack of concentration during training sessions, and high-pitched barking episodes.

I suggested she record a training session and capture the problematic behaviours on film. In the video, I could see Jake running around frantically in the studio and randomly grabbing objects from boxes, opening cupboard doors, and destroying baskets. He would whine and bark during routine training sessions or refuse to execute previously mastered behaviours. Sue made the situation worse because she was insecure and sad in her disorganized environment. She was also frustrated at Jake because of his behaviour. But the problem emanated from Sue's fear of change. We scheduled a session without the dog, during which Sue disclosed information of a more personal nature.

To summarize: Sue was afraid of moving and Jake picked up on her emotions. As mentioned above, bluntly telling people they are the cause of their dog's behaviour problem is counterproductive. The best approach is to guide a person through the disturbance with the use of the mirroring process. Mirroring has a greater psychological, emotional, and behavioural impact on an individual than simple behaviour modification therapy because the immediate result alleviates the emotional upset. Moreover, mirroring serves as a tool people can immediately access and apply.

I asked Sue to recognize the problematic situation as a source of negative emotions. Then I suggested that she needed to stop her reaction to Jake and remove herself from the situation. When a person works with an animal and compromises the relationship, the only possible option is to physically remove the person or dog from the environment. When a person works with people, one can consciously choose to mentally disconnect from the environment without actually leaving.

I suggested to Sue that we both leave the room. This would allow Jake to misbehave on his own. While we were in the other room, I asked Sue to describe the events as they unfolded and summarize, in one word, the entire situation from her perspective. She hesitantly said *confusion*. In answer to the question, "summarize the situation from the dog's point of view," she immediately answered *chaotic*.

When we reunited with Jake, we discussed the recent events in her life and the impact they had on her dog. I asked her how both their lives were similar, what Jake would tell her if he could talk, and what one thing she would change if she could. She initiated the conversation with a sigh and declared that their lives were disorganized and chaotic. She added she was afraid that Jake would not like their new home, would miss his doggy friends, be lonely, and feel totally lost and isolated.

When I asked if she also felt this way about her own life, she began to sob. She admitted that the thought had never crossed her mind until that very moment. Sue felt sad at the thought that she herself might be the source of Jake's behaviour. A deep sense of guilt overwhelmed her. I told her it was OK and that dogs are forever forgiving. I added it was thanks to Jake we were able to put the finger on the problem. Had the dog not been so destructive, Sue might never have dealt with her emotions and suffered from long-lasting emotional scars. I told her Jake was a smart dog because he allowed her to heal and move forward.

The pursuit of self-actualization inevitably initiates transformation and resolution. When Sue realized that her own fear and confusion created the same behaviours in Jake, she immediately stopped reacting and started acting. After a short pause, we started to brainstorm possible training options, leadership development opportunities, and stable emotional involvement. Sue implemented the rigorous social learning, attachment, and training program we designed. The curriculum had three goals aimed at Jake: focus his psychological attention, increase physical wellness, and reduce his destructive behaviour. I instructed Sue to observe Jake on a daily basis and recognize his reactions as her own emotional projection for one week. Because Sue was a trained yoga teacher, I recommended that she meditate and visualize her home environment as a peaceful and relaxed place for her dog.

Meditation is an excellent time to experience positive outcomes in one's own mind: to teach the body, teach the mind. As I uttered that sentence, Jake entered the room with a yoga belt in his mouth. We laughed uncontrollably; clearly, we had a long road ahead of us.

Case study: Ginger

Most dog training facilities do not use social learning and mirroring techniques. In conventional dog training schools, instructors guide dogs in either classical or operant conditioning. Some establishments might council clients through obedience exercises, hoping that their techniques will resolve particular behaviour problems. This approach is the equivalent of treating symptoms without identifying their source. The mirroring and social learning processes between dogs and people address the behaviour problem at the source. One of my long-time clients named Pete and his lovely dog, Ginger, a beautiful ten-year-old neutered female English Springer Spaniel, started to use mirroring and social learning techniques when Ginger was nine-months-old.

Ginger was a very intelligent and enthusiastic puppy. She was toilet trained at three-months-old and never had an accident inside. At six months, Ginger already knew basic obedience commands which she performed with great accuracy. She was a very smart dog, and Peter was a bit overwhelmed with her intellectual needs. One rainy morning in October, I received a call from Peter. He sounded sad, exhausted and frustrated. He explained to me how Ginger had soiled the house twice during the last week, barked at relatives, and constantly tried to jump on people on their daily walks.

Since these were behaviours Ginger had never exhibited before, he was worried. I asked Peter if any changes had occurred in Ginger's environment within the last few weeks. When he replied that nothing had changed and all was well, I then asked him how work was going at his office. This question threw Peter off a little, and he did not answer. Instead, he uttered a long, deep sigh. As it turned out, his law firm had merged and his workload had since doubled. Peter feared he would be unable to fulfil his new duties and felt anxious, confused, and overwhelmed.

I explained to Peter the correlation between his emotional state and Ginger's negative behaviours. I pointed out that his frustration and fear were confusing for Ginger. The once very well-behaved dog was acting out because her environment had changed, and she felt upset. Since Peter could no longer train Ginger or offer her a stable emotional and mental environment, she had begun to act out. Peter immediately saw the connection and asked what he could do. I recommended he find a way to modify his work-related anxiety and a physical outlet to release his own stress. When his negative emotions dissipated, Ginger's negative behaviours would automatically do the same.

A few weeks later, I called Peter for an update. He told me he had transferred a few cases to his colleague and had started to play hockey. He was astounded, as the results had been almost instantaneous. He told me Ginger was back to her normal self. I smiled and giggled a little and hung up the telephone. Peter was happy; Ginger was happy.

Mirroring technique: Ginger

Non-science-based trainers would probably explain Ginger's destructive behaviours as an attempt at dominance and recommend ineffective practices aimed at making the dog submissive. Behaviourism-based trainers might recognize these behaviours as those of a normal dog and treat each problem separately. Typical recommendations would include crate-training to control inappropriate elimination, obedience training for destructive behaviours, and enforced silence after barking. However, social learning and the mirroring technique have many benefits.

First, they offer a simple and affordable therapeutic model readily available to all. Second, individuals who use this approach do not require years of training, nor do they require endless consultation sessions with their clients. Finally, the emotional recovery process has no side effects; healing is continuous in countless circumstances and avoids negative responses in or from other people. Professional behaviour consultants also benefit significantly when they use social learning and mirroring techniques with their clients because trainers tackle behaviour problems at their source. In addition, these techniques function with great accuracy and efficiency, benefitting both client and trainer. Below is an example of how to apply social learning and mirroring.

- Recognize the projection.

  Ginger soiled the house, seems confused about bathroom rules.

- Place an imaginary mirror between you and the dog.

  Ginger is Ginger and Peter is Peter, what am I looking at?

- Take two deep breaths.

  Three would be best.

- Identify the negative emotion.

  Frustration and confusion: I don't like to pick up messes and Ginger seems confused about where the bathroom is.

- Remember that the dog has nothing to do with your reaction.

  Ginger has nothing to do with how I feel. So, how do I feel? I need to mend the conflict with Ginger through positive contact.

- Select and apply a new emotional reaction to the situation.

  I was frustrated, but now I'm happy that Ginger is OK. I accept the situation as it is and will address my confusion separately. Do cognitive game with Ginger to make her feel joyful.

- Leave the situation when change is impossible.

  I cannot change Ginger now, so I will go and meditate. Ginger needs to take a nap while I relax.

You can see how simple it is to change a situation from negative to positive. Later, I will describe the process as an in-depth systematic approach, so you can apply the process to your current life situation. To summarize, we have seen how science and spirituality both define universal energy theory as the governing force. The infinitely small vibrating particles unite to form new and more complex levels of energy. The unification process builds upon and within itself until the condensed energy particles form matter. Consequently, energy and matter can never be separated from one another, for matter is energy organized in different degrees of complexity. Remember the glass globe example that contains the entire universe; if you burn the content of the globe, matter does not disappear; it simply transforms.

Humans and non-human animals are very complex systems, made-up of matter and energy; unfortunately, the increased level of complexity comes at a price: people believe the energy that animates them is unique. As a result, humans psychologically and physically separate themselves from the collective whole. People believe they are one of a kind in every aspect of their persona: body, thought, ideas, knowledge, emotions, and feelings. This belief is nothing more than an illusion, a dream, so to speak. In the alternate reality state, humans, unlike non-human animals, love to demonstrate their uniqueness within groups because it makes them feel complete. The perpetual dichotomy takes form when the expression of the exclusive (divisible) confronts the inclusive (indivisible).

The contradiction escalates into conflict because resolution, in the form of unity, is impossible. There is only one human problem, and it is the belief in separation and its side-effect: guilt, which is always within, never outside ourselves. You will never find peace, joy, wholeness, or love from others because the source of the conflict is the projection itself. In order to solve the dichotomy, the ego invents a clever process: the ego transfers guilt onto the *Id* (Freud, 1933). From the previous seven steps, we can reduce the process to three steps, which represent a shortened version of the previous mirroring technique. I invite you to write your thoughts on the following statements.

- Recognize the problem is not in others, it is within me.

    You can use the seven-step mirroring technique as a start.

- Acknowledge the fact that you have invented the problem.

    People or animals are not responsible for your emotions, you are. That is a fundamental law which no one can escape.

- Accept there was no problem, to begin with, and release it.

Accept, forgive and love yourSelf.

Your answers might have triggered emotions you were not expecting, and that would be quite normal. Actually, the opposite would surprise me. The reason is simple: it is difficult to admit to ourselves that others are not responsible for our emotions. As mentioned previously, the problems you experience are directly related to two singular emotions: fear and love. Every emotion you might use to describe how you feel is a synonym for one or the other of those two.

I remember a case from 2006. The pet caregiver, in this instance, was frustrated because her dog had been defecating inside the house for the last two days. When I asked the client if anything in her immediate environment had changed, or if she had had an emotional exchange with someone recently, she told me the following story. My client had instructed an employee to transfer supplies from one shipping room to another, but the employee had stacked the supplies in the wrong order, to my client's great frustration. The resulting exchange turned into a full-blown argument because he stacked the boxes by category, not by date. I asked her if the arrangement style was relevant to the shipping process. She answered that it was not. Then I asked her why this was making her so angry? She answered *because it was not the way I told him to organize the boxes.*

My client unconsciously perceived the situation as a personal attack on her authority, causing her to fear losing her professionalism, thus affecting her integrity and perceived worth. Consequently, she projected the negative emotion onto her dog, creating a stressful environment, with the result that the stressed dog eliminated inappropriately in the house. Sometimes emotions hide in the unconscious and manifest themselves without our conscious awareness. The goal is to bring negative emotions from the unconscious into the conscious mind, to prevent projections from occurring. The three-step process I describe below is simple to implement, but difficult to achieve in the absence of inner tranquillity. I recommend starting to train your mind before you try to apply the method. Mindful meditation is a practice you should incorporate in your daily activities because it is "A technique of meditation in which distracting thoughts and feelings are not ignored but are rather acknowledged and observed nonjudgmentally" (Moby Medical Dictionary, 2009). Once you are comfortable with mindful meditation, your mirroring skills will improve, and negative projections will decrease.

With mindful meditation, you will recognize that fear and anger can be replaced with positive emotional experiences of joy and wholeness. My goal is to teach you how to awaken from the dream and project loving emotions. Unfortunately, as long as you live, you will be in the dream, but not of the dream. Here are the steps to follow in order to cease the projection and re-connect with yourself and the universal energy: love.

Step 1: Recognizing conflict

The mirroring process allows us to recognize that the problem lies within ourselves, not other people or animals. Step 1 is the most difficult because the person must acknowledge conflict at the fundamental level, the ego. The objective is to re-connect, re-discover, and re-establish your higher self: what I term *yourSelf*. Unfortunately, ego is on a mission to annihilate all forms of happiness, and we have worked hard our entire lives, thus far, to make the concept of unhappiness come true. Psychology even has a term for this self-destructive process; we call it the self-fulfilling prophecy. The ego boycotts our attempts to love, to rejoice, to enjoy life, to experience life.

When happiness fails, ego exults in saying *I told you so* and celebrates victory via destructive behaviours of self-indulgence. All forms of addiction are born within this process and become a vicious cycle of you hate me—I hate you—you are pain—I hate pain—I avoid pain—I avoid you—I avoid me—and then starts over again with you hate me.

The good news is that you can take advantage of your ego to stop the projection cycle. When you find yourself in a situation that triggers annoyance, guilt, fear, frustration, anger, or hostility, you have two choices: to engage or disengage. Everyone can choose to engage in an attack/defend posture or to disengage in a recognize/forgive approach. Free will is a universal law. The forgiveness option is undoubtedly the most difficult part of the process because it requires you to find the point-of-entry and stop the conflict.

The point-of-entry is the opportune moment when one intervenes in a conflict in order to redirect the situation toward a more favourable outcome. Think of the point-of-entry as the size of a door opening inviting one to enter, to step through and start to manage the conflict. You might ask, how do you know if you are in a conflict? If you feel negative emotions, you are in a conflict, even if there is no one in front of you, for you can be in conflict with yourself. If you cannot disengage from the projection and instead become absorbed in the conflict, do not worry, as you can always access the problem later. However, when you are in the moment and cannot leave, the best option is to observe the observer. Try to identify your own actions, reactions, words, lack of words, choice of words, and so on, for this process is the beginning of the second step.

Step 2: Releasing conflict

The mirroring technique teaches us how to disengage from the projection and forgive ourSelves for believing that others are responsible for our experiences, emotions, or choices. To project is to attack and to extend is to forgive. Therefore, the release of ego will be resisted. Resistance then takes the form of anger, not fear because anger protects fear, and fear is the emotion associated with loss: loss of self, loss of life, loss of money, loss of love, loss of worth, loss of face, etc. What better way to make loss disappear than through aggressive displays.

Now I want you to remember the following important sentence: Every time you are in a conflict, the underlying emotion you are experiencing is fear, not anger. You will need a mechanism to recognize which type of fear you are experiencing; I believe the best tool we can use to look at ourSelves is the proverbial mirror—and eventually our dogs. We must acknowledge we have created the conflict out of necessity. The desire to change fear into unconditional love is achievable for everyone, without exception.

Unfortunately, there is no magic solution to the forgiveness process. When you feel disconnected from others, the mirroring technique reminds you who you are. You are not the dog, or the other person, at the physical level; you are everyone and everything on the quantum spectrum. With practice, you will be able to recognize projections more rapidly, thus reducing your intervention times and eventually allowing you to forgive on the spot. For now, you must start with delayed interventions, because you will experience the conflict as it occurs and will not be able to identify which type of fear needs healing. Step 2 will guide you towards gaining command of your emotions through functional and practical exercises. The following exercise starts from a delayed intervention point discussed earlier in the chapter.

The next time you experience a conflict, try to remember as much information as you can from both parties involved and write it down. Pay close attention to emotions. Since you created the conflict, you can learn from it and release it. Once you are in a quiet place, review the scene. But this time, place an imaginary mirror between you and your dog and ask yourSelf the following questions. If the answers do not come right away, be patient with yourself. They are not easy questions to answer as they often trigger undesirable emotions.

Why am I so frustrated, angry, sad, disgusted . . . about this situation?

_____
_____
_____
_____

Why am I reacting so strongly?

_____
_____
_____
_____

Try to identify the fear behind the emotion of anger. Once you identify the underlying source of loss, you should ask yourself the most important question. Take your time and think. Meditate, or engage in some exercise if you need to, as the endorphins naturally relax the body and mind.

If I were my dog, what would I be afraid to lose?

_____
_____
_____
_____

When you attack animals or people, you unconsciously perceive in others the physical, mental, or emotional characteristics you dislike in yourself, and the recognition of those inadequacies leads to fear. As mentioned before, the ultimate fear is death. At this stage, ask yourself these last two questions.

How can I change the negative emotion into a positive feeling?

_____
_____
_____
_____

How can I transform division into unity?

_____
_____
_____

You will soon realize you have created the conflict in order to heal yourSelf. Projections stop when you answer these questions because the answers will always yield the same response, forgiveness. If projection creates perception, extension undoubtedly creates forgiveness.

Step 3: Forgiving conflict

Forgiveness is your life's purpose. In fact, it is everybody's life purpose because we are all connected. When you accomplish forgiveness, you no longer need to project your emotions and feelings onto your dog, or other humans, because you will no longer experience fear. Once you have forgiven yourSelf, you will no longer believe separation from the universal energy is possible. But first, you will need an action plan to learn how to forgive.

Now that you have seen how to recognize and mirror conflicts, you will establish acceptance, the process by which one moves from passive to active forgiveness. Passive forgiveness takes place when ego surrenders or plays god during a conflict, to rid itself of guilt. In this form of acceptance, ego loves *if, and only if,* other people act a certain way. Active forgiveness occurs when spirit loves others *in spite of* their actions during the same conflict.

The difference is that love extends and creates forgiveness for both yourSelf and others. The active form is recognition and acceptance. The *how can I change division into unity* question can only be answered with one word, acceptance. When you accept your dog is not responsible for your emotions or feelings, you have in part accepted and reclaimed your projections. Now, forgiveness becomes the new strategy.

Here is an exercise to practice. Sit towards the sunlight in a comfortable chair. Close your eyes and take three deep breaths. Allow your body to sink into the chair and connect with the floor, the building foundation, and the earth below you. You will feel heavy at this stage, but the feeling will subside quickly. Throughout the following steps, try to look out through the space between your eyebrows where the bridge of your nose begins. NOTE: keep your eyes closed while you direct them towards the sunlight, but do not stare directly at the sun.

On a ten-point scale, ten being the worst feeling and zero being the best, evaluate how you generally feel before your meditation session. With the number in mind, visualize a bubble made of light, step into it, and repeat *I forgive you*, as many times as necessary, until you feel lighter. You may feel the urge to smile, so go ahead and release the joy. Once you feel peaceful, bring your attention back to your body. Now, slowly return to your body, wiggle your fingers and toes around, and breathe deeply. Slowly look away from the sun before opening your eyes just a little. The colours might seem off. You will notice everything around you is the same greenish-gray colour. We call this neural adaptation or sensory adaptation (Schacter et al., 2015), and it is normal. Allow your eyes to focus and regain normal colour sensation before you open them further. This process might take a few minutes.

Re-evaluate how you feel after the session. The number should have decreased and you should feel less angry and more joyful. Do not worry about the number per say, but rather concentrate on how much lighter you feel. The sooner after the conflict you repeat these steps, the better you will become at on-the-stop forgiveness. The mirroring goal is to accept the dog, or person, with whom you were in conflict as neutral. True forgiveness heals projection and creates extension. Once you forgive the dog, you will have in fact forgiven yourSelf. Remember, universal energy is indivisible; hence, you can only, truly, forgive yourSelf. To live without fear is to experience life at the most fundamental level, unity. A return to the *Essential Essence* is humanity's goal (Walsch, 2017).

Case study: Marmaduke

Marmaduke, a two-year-old neutered male Great Dane, was a fearful dog who on occasion could be aggressive. His owner, Peter, was an extrovert who loved the outdoors and all things new. Peter adopted Marmaduke when he was a year old, from a local shelter. Peter was excited to show off his new bud, but Marmaduke would pull away from people each chance he got. Not long after the adoption, Peter noticed Marmaduke would become aggressive when he tried to socialize him. So he came to me with a very specific complaint: Marmaduke bites. Peter and I discussed his case, and I gave him homework. He was to answer the following three questions as honestly as possible; the following are his answers.

- Recognize the problem is not in the dog, it is within me.

- How does Marmaduke make you feel generally?

    Marmaduke makes me angry because I can't fit in with my friends.
- Acknowledge the fact that you have invented the problem.

- Describe in one sentence which emotion Marmaduke triggers in you?

    I want to fit in and I don't want to be left out because it makes me feel rejected.
- Accept there was no problem, to begin with, and release it.

- Before Marmaduke came into your life, did you ever feel rejected?

All the time. I know he doesn't want to fit in, so I guess I'll let go of my wish for him to be a social butterfly.

After the process, Peter finally accepted Marmaduke as he was and was able to enjoy his furry friend, and I am happy to report, Peter was never bitten again, nor were his friends. I bumped into Peter a few years ago and asked him how Marmaduke was. Answering the three questions I had asked him had made him think about his own life, and how the need to fit in had taken control. He recognized his patterns in Marmaduke, and the dog helped him achieve his dream. Peter had always wanted to travel across Canada with his dog, and so he did. Sadly, Marmaduke died on the journey.

The story does not end there. Peter was lucky to find puppy Scoobydoo, who grew up to be a highly social dog, not because Peter forced him, but because Peter properly socialized his puppy during a critical period of development. I never met Scoobydoo, but if he is anything like my Great Dane Ethan, the entire community loved him.

Dog socialization during the critical period of development is very important and is explained by social-cognitive learning theory. The next chapter of this book is dedicated to the prevention of problematic, dysfunctional, and deviant behaviours in dogs. Research on social learning in dogs is relatively new, but the study of attachment and social imitation learning in dogs is on the verge of a major shift. And since social-cognitive learning theory is an emerging field of research on canines, no book on dog behaviour modification should go without a chapter on the topic. I ask you to open your mind, let go of assumptions, and read attentively what follows. You can even try, as we go along, to practice social-cognitive learning with your dog, for there are no risks to your furry friend or yourself. On the contrary, your dog might like you even more.

The real questions are, what do you treasure, and how much do you treasure it? Once you have learned to consider these questions and bring them into all your actions, you will have little difficulty in clarifying the means. (ACIM, 2007, T-2.II.3:5)

Reader notes

Chapter 6: Social-Cognitive Learning Theory

Attachment theory

For the sake of this chapter, I will refer to the attachment formed between dogs and humans, unless otherwise specified. Attachment is the emotional link formed between a parental figure and its offspring (Lorenz, 1954); between a mother and a child (Bowlby, 1969); between a bitch and her pup during a critical period of development (Scott & Fuller, 1965).

Attachment serves as a species-specific survival mechanism, and a strategy for communication, emotional development, and to some extent conflict management. Without attachment, an organism would soon perish. Konrad Lorenz influenced Bowlby with his work on imprinting:

> *In its narrow usage, the term is tied tightly to Lorenz's original ideas about imprinting (1935). In his early papers Lorenz not only called attention to the fact that in many species of bird attachment behaviour comes quickly to be focused on a particular object, or class of objects, but postulated also that the process whereby that occurred had unique properties: 'imprinting has a number of features which distinguish it fundamentally from a learning process. It has no equal in the psychology of any other animal, least of all a mammal.* (Bowlby, 1969, p. 166)

In his book, *A Secure Base: Parent-child Attachment and Healthy Human Development*, Bowlby (1988) mentions "Historically the theory [attachment] was developed out of the object-relations tradition in psychoanalysis; but it has drawn also on concepts from evolution theory, ethology, control theory, and cognitive psychology" (p. 119). Bowlby and Ainsworth developed the theory further to propose a secure attachment and three insecure types of attachment: ambivalent, avoidant, and disorganized (Bretherton, 1992). In a secure attachment, pair-bonded individuals can form sincere relationships, demonstrate empathy, establish suitable boundaries, and explore environmental stimuli.

Securely attached children and adults are confident they will receive positive emotional feedback should they require assistance during stressful or anxious events from their environments or immediate surroundings. Parents of securely attached children are mentally and emotionally available, connected, and supportive. Secure adults form empathetic, intimate, understanding and affectionate relationships (Bowlby, 1969, 1988).

Children and adults with insecure ambivalent styles of attachment are anxious, apprehensive, controlling, accusing, charming, or unreliable. Their relationships are often conflictual and emotionally unpredictable. These types of relationships repeatedly turn into negatively charged emotional vicious cycles because parents of ambivalent children tend to become emotionally and mentally inconsistent adults. The pattern continues into adulthood, and relationships become an emotional roller coaster, thus continuing the cycle. It is common to see avoidant and ambivalent styles in relationships, for individuals project their respective style onto each other, and these, in turn, confirm the attachment they have experienced as children.

The insecure avoidant attachment style is self-explanatory: individuals avoid emotional relationships and intimacy. Pair-bonded individuals are often distant, critical, strict, harsh, intolerant, and inflexible. The original attachment style offered by the parental figure was most likely unavailable or rejecting. Children who face stressful or anxious events cannot turn to their parent for emotional support or reassurance. Unable to cope, children feel unequipped to deal with stressful situations; consequently, as adults, they will avoid future social situations or emotional relationships.

The last form of insecure attachment refers to disorganized connections. As the title implies, people with this style of attachment demonstrate disorganized behaviour. Terms used to describe their emotional relationships include: tumultuous, chaotic, insensitive, explosive, volatile, abusive, and untrusting yet craving of security. Inconsistencies in intimacy and social conduct make it difficult for people with disorganized attachments to form enduring relationships. It is common to see people with a disorganized attachment bounce from one relationship to the next. C. Rees adds "Safe independence is unlikely and criminality in adulthood common without recovery." (2012, p.187). Many adults with this style of attachment acquire animals to help fill the emotional void and soothe the psychological pain; unfortunately, comfort soon turns to distress between human and animal.

Ádám Miklósi, Department of Ethology, Eötvös University, Budapest, Hungary, and his team have also researched dog attachment and come up with the same results as Ainsworth (Topál et al., 1998). In their paper, *Attachment Behavior in Dogs (Canis familiaris): A New Application of Ainsworth's (1969) Strange Situation Test*, Topál and his colleagues (p. 219) concluded "A dog's relationship to humans is analogous to child-parent and chimpanzee-human attachment behavior because the observed behavioral phenomena and the classification are similar to those described in mother-infant interactions." Attachment is a vital component between individuals, humans or non-humans, for, without a positive connection, communication and learning are problematic.

It can be difficult to develop a secure attachment with an older dog, especially if your canine companion was improperly socialized during the critical period of social development, and even more so if the dog has emotional scars.

The positive result of a successful period of social development directly influences resilience, or the capacity to recover quickly from difficult situations. Consequently, secure attachments serve to facilitate adaptation during stressful situations.

Securely attached dogs rely on their owners' positive feedback to investigate novel stimuli; consequently, resilience will develop as dogs become better equipped at dealing with new situations. Later, should a similar incident or stimulus trigger negative emotions, dogs will turn to their humans for guidance, approval, and problem-solving tools. Conversely, if dogs are unable to manage their emotions and reach their resilience threshold, humans must remove dogs from these problematic situations and allow the dogs to return to an emotionally functional level. Note, I did not write normal level; I wrote functional level.

The shake behaviour, not to be confused with trembling, is a good indicator the animal has returned to a lower arousal state and can start to learn and manage their emotions once more. Insecure attachments directly affect resilience levels. Individuals who have not learned to cope with stressors are more likely to avoid novel stimuli; thus, develop lower resilience thresholds (Zeanah, 1990).

Bowlby, Banduras, Miklósi, and other researchers tend to reach a similar conclusion: social learning between humans, or humans and dogs, requires a social connection, a favourable environment, and the ability to process, store and retrieve information. The three criteria directly influence attachment because emotions are at the root of learning. Just think of how your favourite—or least favourite—topic in school made you feel, and you will grasp the relationship between attachment and social-cognitive learning. Bandura illustrated the social-cognitive learning process with a triangle (Figure 9), which is an excellent visual tool to help understand the process.

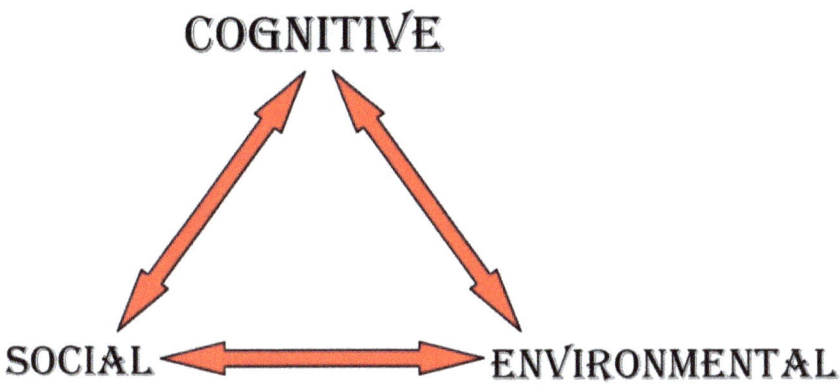
Figure 9. Social-cognitive triangle.

Social learning

Why did Bandura represent the social-cognitive learning theory with a triangle and not a circle? It might seem intuitive to think of attachment and social-cognition as a circular model. Unfortunately, a sphere cannot represent the multi-directional exchange, which occurs between cognition, the environment, and social interaction. In short, the social-cognitive theory is an interconnected bi-directional exchange model of learning. To quote Bandura, "Social cognitive theory favours a model of causation involving triadic reciprocal determinism. In this model of reciprocal causation, behaviour, cognition and other personal factors, and environmental influences all operate as interacting determinants that influence each other bidirectionally" (Bandura, 1989, p.2).

Motivation and anticipation directly link to the social-cognitive model because the outcome of behaviour is dependent on self-efficacy and reinforcement. Self-esteem and wellness increase when people believe they have control over their skills and the environment in which they evolve. Perceived control also applies to non-human animals.

Dogs that perceive they have a sense of control over their bodies and the environment are normally psychologically well adjusted. Ellen Skinner (1996) suggests, "Control is important to psychological functioning" (p.549). The social-cognitive learning theory model is best understood when we look at each component individually. According to Bandura (1989), triadic reciprocal determinism is presented as B = behaviour, P = cognition, and E = environment.

Social determinants

The social element of the triangle reflects behaviour, for it is where attachments form and create relationships. Individuals bring their own sets of physical, intellectual, and biological experiences to the relationship, and these indirectly influence one another. Human and dog emotions, thoughts, beliefs, expectations, and intentions are elements that compose the social interaction within the relationship. Attachment serves another important role in our interspecies relationships: communication. When dogs securely attach to a person, they look to that person for feedback on how to solve problems. In fact, they are the only animal species that look at people for information (Miklosi, Topal & Csanyi, 2004).

Mirror neurons and imitation, either as related or unrelated processes, both influence behaviour; consequently, our role as information bearers is vital for efficient interspecies communication (Rizzolatti & Fabbri-Destro, 2008; Gallese et al., 2011). In their research on imitation, Fugazza and Miklósi (2015) discuss a *side effect*, if you will, of social learning through imitation.

> *Importantly, this study clearly demonstrates that the use of social learning with the Do as I do method enhances dogs' memory of the trained actions and their verbal cues, when dogs are required to perform in a context that is different from that where*

the training took place, thus it enhances generalization. (p.11).

Memory increases problem-solving skills and helps dogs to generalize their behaviours within different environments. In my experience as a social learning teacher, dogs acquire knowledge faster, behaviours are more reliable in changing environments, and dogs display novel behaviours more frequently. Within the social determinant element, we must consider biological factors. Non-human animals come with sets of internal desires; unfortunately, we can only observe the result of desire once the animal exhibits the behaviours associated with it. We cannot evaluate the length of time the animal was experiencing the desire; consequently, the ability to learn diminishes when a desire remains unsatisfied.

Imagine that you have to learn a new security code for the computer system at work, but your body tells you *I have a pressing urge to urinate* at that exact moment. Chances are you will not be able to learn or retain the new information. You must satisfy the biological need to urinate first in order to proceed with learning. Maslow's hierarchy of needs pyramid (Boyd, Bee, and Johnson, 2009) states that biological needs and desires must be satisfied in order to learn. The pyramid of needs includes breathing, hunger, thirst, reproduction, thermo-regulation, elimination, and rest.

This is probably the hardest determinant to evaluate because most non-human animal internal mechanisms are alien to us. If you think about it, dogs have a brain; therefore, dogs must suffer from an occasional headache. Every dog caregiver can attest to the following statement *What's wrong with you today?!* or *He's not normally like this, I don't know what's got into him?!*

When Albear does not execute previously mastered behaviours, I jokingly say he must have a headache today. My point is that we need to be constantly aware of how biology plays an important part in learning. We cannot simply assume dogs refuse to listen because they are hard-headed. I remember a student training session not long ago: the dog decided he no longer wanted to learn, and the student got frustrated.

I asked the student what she thought was wrong, but she did not know. I suggested she go back to basics: breathing, food, toilet, thermo-regulation, thirst, etc. The student took the dog out first. It relieved itself immediately, ran back inside to the training spot, and resumed the session. Sometimes, a dog just needs to go to the bathroom. It was a lesson well learned. Even hunger can render an animal uncooperative. My policy is, never starve an animal before a training session because one day, you might be on the menu.

Cognitive determinants

P stands for cognitive because, in reality, two separate beings come together each with *personal* cognitive characteristics. Human and non-human pairs are composed of distinctive sets of biological sensory organs and brain functions. Cognitively speaking, sensory perception and transduction are different between humans and dogs. Cognitive processing varies; our physical abilities are poles apart, and we speak different languages. So why do we live in a symbiotic relationship with dogs?

The answer is because we complement each other within our social and cognitive attributes. We define cognition as the mental processes involved in acquiring information, knowledge and understanding (Schacter et al., 2015). Cognition also includes encoding and retrieving information or knowledge at specific moments and for specific purposes. Retrieving information involves remembering, judging and problem-solving.

Obviously, memory plays an important role in cognition. In psychology, we divide memory into three: Sensory, short-term, and long-term (Schacter et al., 2015). Sensory memory occurs through your sensory organs: skin, eyes, ears, mouth, and nose and lives for approximately one second in the brain. Short-term memory regroups a limited amount of information that normally is short-lived. Frequent recollection is required to keep the information retrievable. In humans, the short-term memory lasts approximately sixty seconds. Conversely, dogs can only store information in their short-term memory for approximately 15 seconds (Chance, 2008). Based on my experience, 15 seconds is the average short-term memory for dogs. Just like short-term memory, the dog will need to recall long-term memories for them to remain active in the brain. Once they recall and reprocess memories, dogs need to sleep after learning for memory consolidation to occur (Kis et al., 2017).

Long-term memory regroups two categories: implicit and explicit. Implicit memory involves the unconscious, or the part of memory that we do not control. Implicit memory includes procedural memory that is responsible for storing repetitive skills such as walking, driving a car, or riding a bicycle. In other words, implicit procedural means it is part of you; you no longer have to think about the steps necessary to drive your car; you just know out of habit. Implicit memory also stores conditioned emotional responses (CER) and conditioned reflexes (Schacter et al., 2015).

Explicit memory is a little more complex (Figure 10). Explicit memory is the conscious memory. We divide explicit memory into two major segments: episodic and semantic. Our life events and experiences are stored in the episodic memory, while facts and concepts are stored in our semantic memory. When you remember facts for an exam, you are accessing your semantic memory (McGill, 2016). When you remember family, friends, colleagues, or social events filled with emotions, you are engaging your episodic memory. According to Fugazza, Pógány & Miklósi (2016), dogs seem to possess an episodic memory similar to humans. In their words, "Therefore, this form of memory in non-human animals is referred to as *episodic-like memory.*" (p.1). Obviously, I am oversimplifying how the brain works, as this is not a book on neuroscience.

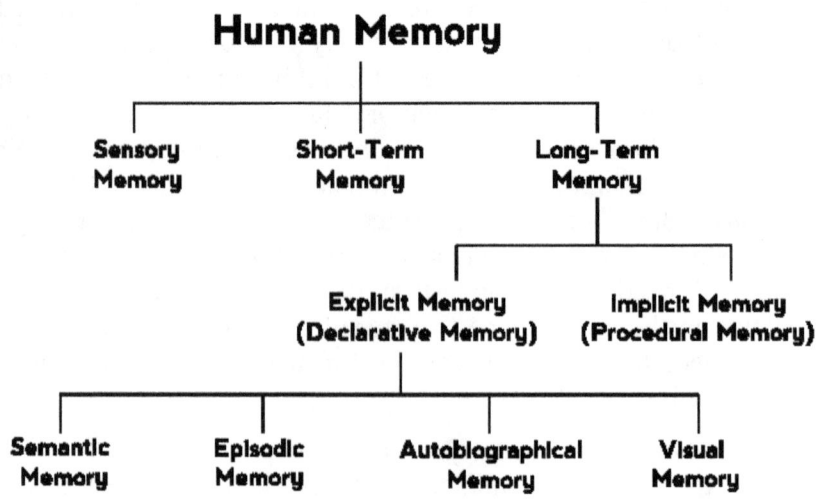

Figure 10. Human memory.

Behaviourism is part of cognition within the social-cognitive system, for it is a fundamental part of learning. Classical and operant conditioning influence memory through associations and repetitions; therefore, behaviourism and social-cognitivism occur simultaneously. I know some purists will frown and claim that is sheer humbug! But before you are tempted to agree, let me explain how social-cognitive learning theory and behaviourism work. The cognitive determinant is part of the bidirectional exchange between the environment and behaviour. The environment will change according to the behaviour dogs and humans express within the environment; thus, the environment changes as they modify their behaviour. Think of a circular cycle where one keeps modifying the other: Environment => Behaviour => Environment => Behaviour (Bandura, 1989).

In behaviourism, dogs and humans make associations between stimuli and behaviour and draw their conclusions based on the positive or negative outcome of those associations. Positive consequences increase the likelihood behaviours will occur again, and negative consequences decrease the likelihood behaviours will occur again. It is a simple process when you think about it. Imagine you are late on the first day of your dream job and as you rush towards the stairs to get to the office, you break your ankle. From this situation, we can make simple life-changing associations: either not to wear high heels to work or be on time for work, if you wish to increase the likelihood you will keep your job.

Dogs continuously make similar associations. A dog can make a connection between any two things: for example, I drop things so frequently that my dog Albear has made the connection between me + broom = loud *banging* sound. Like all dogs learn in all environments, and sometimes involuntarily acquire undesirable behaviours, my dog developed a fear of the broom. In the following section, I will explore the last determinant: the relationship between social and environmental characteristics.

Environmental determinants

The E in the triangular Figure 8 relates to the environment. As previously discussed, the surroundings influence both social and behavioural determinants because of their direct impact on biology and cognition. Brain stimulation via cognitive games and exercises directly interacts with the social determinant, which in turn, favours attachment. The cognitive determinant also directly interacts with the environmental component because over or under stimulating environments inhibit learning. Yet, cognitive reciprocal determinism, which occurs between behaviour and the environment, allows dogs to learn regardless of the environmental conditions.

Let me explain. Imagine a room a few degrees too cool; would you be able to learn efficiently or would your mind focus on how to get warm? A simple two-degree variation in temperature means an organism will focus solely on thermoregulation and the mind will not concentrate and learn (Bandura, 1989). It is the attachment (social) and the ability to learn (cognition) that allow an organism to adapt to an unfavourable environment. The ability to adapt and function under stressful conditions increases resilience. In canids, age, sex, health, hunger, social status, and size characteristics influence group dynamics because of environmental stimuli.

The same goes for humans. Pet caregivers do not have the same relationship with their dogs as trainers, groomers, veterinarians, technicians, or pet sitters because emotions and the environment do not influence their professional perception. If an owner is anxious and projects anxiety, professionals, on the other hand, will have a better relationship with the dog because they are not projecting anxiety. I project my emotions on my own dog because of my attachment to him; conversely, I do not project on my clients' dogs because my expectations are lower than those of the owner (Bandura, 1977).

In other words, I expect results, but I do no put an emotional value on the outcome. In my experience, the most favourable environment that predisposes an animal to learn, regardless of stimuli, is one that includes a securely attached human. If an animal learns how to learn and finds itself in the presence of a secure human attachment, stimuli in the environment can be overwhelming, yet not fully detrimental to learning.

My favourite example occurred a few years back. Albear and I were sitting on the balcony in front of the Dogue Shop when a flash protest crept up on us. Within seconds, protesters banging on pots and pans surrounded Albear and me. There was no way we could escape. Albear is still afraid of drum and drum-like noises, which meant the next ten minutes could potentially traumatize him, yet again. I immediately called him over and started to work on our easy behaviour repertoire. Albear knew the commands: left paw, right paw, kiss, up, double high-five, turn, sit, talk, down, and so many more. I did a warm-up with the easy behaviours and moved to complex skills. That afternoon, right there on the balcony, Albear learned to sneeze on command.

Albear is not a particularly smart dog, but he has learned how to learn, which makes him a highly determined worker. As the pendulum finishes swinging from the extreme left of punishment to the far right of reinforcement only, social-cognitive learning theory brings animal training into the twenty-first century because it balances out behaviourism poles. Social-cognitive learning will improve inter-species relationships, facilitate communication, accelerate training, and promote less invasive, complex, and pricey protocols for pet caregivers.

> *You cannot know how to respond to what you do not understand. Be tempted not in this, and yield not to the ego's triumphant use of empathy for its glory.* (ACIM, 2007, T-16.I.4:6)

Reader notes

Chapter 7: The Big Picture - SCAT

Separation: Birth of the ego

Thus far, we have examined universal energy, projection, mirroring, and social-cognitive learning theories. Operant and classical conditioning also influence behaviour. But behaviourism on its own cannot account for imitation, because a secure social connection is required. Science likes to study individual components or structures of life. In psychology or neurobiology, research tries to discover and explain how certain parts of the brain function. The downside of science is that our global understanding of a specific topic gets lost.

As a young emerging scientist, I like to see the big picture in everything. In other words, where science divides, I unite. Consequently, the final section of this book will focus on unifying the content of previous chapters into one coherent process, which I refer to as SCAT: Social Cognitive Attachment Training.

As you now know, it all begins with projection. When you think about it, both ego and the universe project outwards and create what we perceive as reality, yet without sensory organs; **nothing unreal exists**, which makes sense, for, without a body, the ego cannot perceive what is not there, or what is unreal. *A Course in Miracles* also reminds us that we project our ego into the world to validate the insane idea that we are separate from one another, and thus, from the universal energy. The frightening images we perceive confirm the idea: separation is real and scary.

Without ego and its projected unreal existence, there is no separation and no fear. When spirit returns to the source of universal energy, **nothing real can be threatened**. At the quantum level, wholeness can never be made separate; real can never be unreal; everything can never be no-thing. Similarly, the rules apply at the spiritual level. Spirit only knows love;

truth only generates peace; forgiveness leads to unity and extension. Everything you experience is a projection from the ego onto a world you then perceive as real. Ego has one simple objective: to keep you from remembering and believing that unity is your true identity. In other words, the self-fulfilling prophecy by which you set your mind-body connection up to fail, to prove to your spirit you are no good; and since you ultimately fail, ego perpetuates the cycle with inner monologues such as *I told you so!* or *you'll never be good enough!* Ego's purpose is to keep you believing that separation is true; that we are separate from one another and from universal energy. The belief that separation is true creates negative emotions, which in turn allow negative thoughts to occur.

Eventually, people express their inner monologues through self-destructive behaviours. Human-dog relationships are no different from human-human affiliations. We project onto dogs, and in the same manner, we project onto people. Therefore, to identify projections, ask yourself the following questions. Be honest, this process is about you, for You.

What am I angry at…?
_____
_____
_____

How does this apply to me?
_____
_____
_____

What am I afraid of losing?
_____
_____
_____
_____

Why does fear feel real?

_____

_____

_____

_____

    You might notice physical symptoms while you answer the above questions, but do not worry; that is normal since the ego and the body are connected. The body cannot live without the ego; consequently, the ego will fight back in protest. Symptoms can range from mild headaches to migraines, nausea, fatigue, muscle contractions, spasms, dizziness, frustration, and confusion, to name a few. Once you finish the introspection process, you will feel lighter, and your thoughts will be clearer. Overall, you will feel happier because you will experience peace; for, if the ego is born out of the belief that separation from the universal energy is real, then unification resolves the conflict.

    The universal dichotomy contains oppositions because one cannot exist without the other; yet universal energy is all there is because it cannot be separate from itself, for it simply is. When ego takes over the mind-body connection, ideas of separation begin to emerge. The birth of ego corresponds to adolescence. The term adolescence dates back to the 13th century and corresponds to the transition phase between childhood and adolescence. Psychologist Erik Erikson calls adolescence the period during which the identity is formed (Boyd, Bee & Johnson, 2009, p.29). Simply put, adolescence is the period when the body and mind become the seat of ego.

    In the Mādhyamika philosophy—the doctrine of ultimate emptiness—the connectedness between the dependant (real) and independent (unreal) is described as a cosmic force pouring into itself, "since there is no dharma[10] whatsoever that is not dependently originated, therefore there is no dharma whatsoever that is not empty." (Arnold, n.d.). Nāgārjuna defines the Mādhyamika philosophy as the intermediate path or

---

10 In Hinduism, the principle of cosmic order.

the middle way between what is real and unreal. The Mādhyamika philosophy dates back to the second century A.D. during a time when quantum physics was neither a science nor an idea. The Encyclopaedia Britannica summarizes the philosophy perfectly:

> *The world is a cosmic flux of momentary interconnected events (dharmas), however, the reality of these events might be viewed. Nāgārjuna sought to demonstrate that the flux itself could not be held to be real, nor could the consciousness perceiving it, as it itself is part of this flux.* (Arnold, 1998).

The concept of a universal energy dates back even further. During the Egyptian New Kingdom, Tuthmosis I, Hatshepsut, and later Amenhotep II directly chose to represent or associate themselves with the sun god Aten (Aldred, 1991; Morenz, 1973). The Aten refers back to the sun god Ra as the spirit creator of the world and giver of life (Hill, 2010). Neferneferuaten Nefertiti and her husband Amenhotep IV, later known as Akhenaten, transformed Egyptian spiritual beliefs as being completely identified with the sun god. Akhenaten and Nefertiti both believed in one divine force guiding the world: the Aten. Akhenaten's worship of Ra-Amun-Horus "was based on the scientific observation that the sun's energy is the ultimate source of all life." (Hill, 2010). The belief in one deity, one universal force, only lasted throughout the New Kingdom, but the idea became prevalent during the reign of Akhenaten.

If our distant ancestors believed in one unified energy theory, I sometimes wonder why modern day science and many religious doctrines refuse to recognize that they are in harmony in the quest for god as the universal energy. Our experience as expressions of a universal energy includes the experience of the body, not the misinterpretation of the mind;

furthermore, since we give birth to ego during adolescence, surely adulthood is the period when we can dismantle it, for adulthood is the period of *prudent self-control*. Again, according to Erik Erikson, we experience three periods of development during adulthood: Intimacy vs. Isolation, Generativity vs. Stagnation, and Ego Integrity vs. Despair (Boyd, Bee & Johnson, 2009).

If his phrase "ego integrity" means how you integrate ego, we can understand this as the process by which we unite with the spirit as our guiding force. If one cannot join spirit and become one with life, then the resulting despair generates fear of death later on. All the theories and exercises we have discussed so far have one point in common: cease to believe in separation and start to experience unity. I am simply adding the dog to the equation to facilitate the process of unification with the universal energy, or if you prefer, god.

Unification: Birth of the spirit

I believe our spirit, mind, and body is the expression of the universal energy manifested from a successive layering of particles, each still connected to the source. Consequently, we cannot observe subatomic particles apart from themselves. Quantum entanglement and spin experiments demonstrate just how interconnected particles are. When researchers affect the spin direction of one particle, the second particle automatically spins in the other direction (Bartlett, 2015).

The dichotomy is not only a universal rule; opposites are universal truths. The collective unconsciousness is a direct result of the interconnectedness of morphic resonance build-ups. Einstein, Jung, Sheldrake, M-theory, and spiritual scriptures all have one thing in common; a universal energy governs the universe, the world, and our place in it. It is an unavoidable and inescapable truth.

Spirit does not have a birthplace, for love as a universal energy cannot be less than it is. Neither can a universal force, which simultaneously drives everything and nothing, be equal to more than it is. Therefore, if the birth of ego stems from fear, and spirit originates directly from love, where does the human experience fit into the grand scheme of things? We manifest into a body to experience the ultimate truth, for knowledge without experience is simply incomplete. Here is an example. The mind can know red; however, it is an entirely different experience to see red.

Without the human body and senses, we cannot experience knowledge in its fundamental expression. For spirit to know love, it must experience non-love, and as long as ego is in control, we experience non-love as fear. Although ego is necessary for our physical survival, it is possible to remove negative conditioning from the mind. The deconditioning process can be scary, uncomfortable, and even cause physical discomfort. However, spiritual growth is the only path to enlightenment and true happiness.

Einstein described perfectly how the universe works when he gave the snow globe example in the first chapter. Nothing is created without its opposite; hence, when we unconsciously allow our ego to dominate our thoughts, spirit never disappears; it simply becomes quieter and much harder to *hear*, figuratively speaking. The surrender of ego will improve your human and dog interaction because spirit becomes the dominant thought force that extends outward. From here on, ego turns into the physical executor, or what I call, the body driver.

My favourite analogy illustrates the concept a little better: your body is a car, your ego is the driver, and everything else around the car is the spirit. Although spirit controls the universe around the car, it cannot actually drive the car. When the ego is quiet, spirit can become the co-driver and change the experience. Yet in the physical world, the car itself remains unreal to spirit. Spirit still needs ego to drive the car as it moves forward in the physical world. When the car rusts and ceases to function, the driver may seem to die along with it, but the driver was never apart from the car and therefore, was never real.

Spirit never rusts and ceases to function, for spirit was never a part of the car or driver. Spirit is simply the universal force driving everything forward. If I have said it before, I am saying it again, *you are not in the world; you are of the world.*

The hard part of our journey is to silence ego and let spirit do the co-driving, or guiding if you prefer. I know the path can seem difficult at first, but it gets easier. As you embark on the spiritual superhighway, you will realize you are not alone. In reality, every single human on earth is on the same journey. Once you realize we are all in this together, you will start to extend and influence other *drivers*. If you have this book in your hands, the journey has already begun for you and your dog. To that fact, I must briefly express my sincere gratitude for your open-mindedness. You are one brave person if you can admit that you and your dog need guidance on the path of life.

A quote from Mohawk chief Dan George on animals reminds me just how important the human-animal bond is, and explains why I chose to walk the path *"If you do not talk to them [animals], you will not know them, and what you do not know, you will fear. What one fears, one destroys."* I have kept those words in my mind since childhood, and they eventually led me to realize how a simple word or phrase can have an immeasurable impact on someone. One word can call spirit to rise and ego to subside. That is the miracle. That is our purpose. As Emily Dickinson (1924) wrote:

> *We never know how high we are, till we are called to rise;*
>
> *And then, if we are true to plan, our statures touch the skies.*
>
> *The Heroism we recite would be a daily thing,*
>
> *Did not ourselves the Cubits warp, for fear to be a King.*

Let me reassure you, we are all kings, for the opposite of ego is pure creative potential. The extension of creativity facilitates relationships, makes the body feel lighter, clears the mind, puts an end to projection, gives rise to extension, and increases your ability to train your dog objectively. From a human perspective, simple ailments disappear and breath deepens. From a canine perspective, communication is clearer and behaviour improves. As your guide on this spiritual and behavioural path through mirroring your dog projections, let me offer a few tools you can take home, so to speak, and use with your dog and other humans. Fill in the following statements with experiences you have had in the past that closely resemble the affirmation.

I offered unconditional forgiveness

_____
_____
_____
_____

I purposefully chose a positive outcome

_____
_____
_____
_____

I have truly given without wanting anything in return

_____
_____
_____
_____

I have loved mySelf unconditionally

_____
_____
_____
_____

Do your answers make you feel light, happy, content, and joyful? Or, conversely, do your answers make you feel fearful, anxious, stressed, or angry? Write your feelings and thoughts; you might want to refer back to them later. Meanwhile, remember enlightenment brings spiritual growth, for to become enlightened means to extend love, spiritual knowledge, or insight to someone. Consequently, if you enlighten others through love, you have in fact given yourSelf love. As the rule of dichotomy states: to give is to receive.

The Social-Cognitive Attachment Training (SCAT) model unifies dog training, behaviour modification, and human psychology (see Figure 14). The process transforms insecure attachments into secure ones through mirroring and the application of cognitive exercises. SCAT will give you concrete tools you can bring anywhere and everywhere.

But first, let me enumerate the steps and explain them in the following case studies. You can try the exercises with your dog and test your relationship. Actually, I highly recommend that you try the exercises with your dog and note any changes in its behaviour, and in your own. I have included a summary definition for each step to facilitate your recollection of information from previous chapters.

1. *Projection*

Definition: humans defend themselves against their own unconscious impulses or qualities (both positive and negative) by denying their existence in themselves while attributing them to others.

Try to observe the observer and describe a recent event you want to analyze.

2. *Mirroring*

Definition: the unconscious replication of another person or animal's nonverbal signals through mirror neurons.

Once you have written the event, you can ask yourself these questions:

I hate it when…

I am upset because….

I am afraid of losing…

I am angry at…

3. Test attachment type

Definition: all four attachment styles (three insecure + one secure) are the result of early interactions with the mother or primary caregiver during the first 18 months of a child's life or 16 weeks in a dog's life.

Ask a SCAT professional to help you conduct Ainsworth's strange situation test between you and your dog.

4. Cognitive exercise

Definition: training that reflects the hypothesis that cognitive abilities maintain or improve with brain exercise.

Brain Games are activities on different levels, which build trust, enhance learning abilities, and problem-solving skills within the human-dog pair.

5. Social exercise

Definition: social exercises relate to the experience, behaviour, and interaction of persons forming groups for the purpose of promoting companionship.

Play social-cognitive Brain Games, test yawning, stretching, massage your dog, cuddle, or conduct socially bonding training exercises such as touching.

6. Imitation

Definition: imitation is an advanced training method whereby an individual or animal observes and replicates another's behaviour.

You will need the help of a professional trainer qualified in social learning to teach the following behaviours.

Yawn, stretch, wave, high-five, circle, and calm.

7. Training

Definition: a trainer teaches a human or non-human a skill, ability, or behaviour using behaviourism and/or social-cognitive learning theory.

Identify the target behaviour the human will need to learn, demonstrate the behaviour, and reinforce new responses in the person and subsequently the dog.

Practice training exercises regularly.

Case study: George

When I met George, he was a 6-month-old neutered, male, mixed breed dog with a lot of energy and spunk. The puppy was rambunctious in the house and reactive to other dogs, but not aggressive. His owner was a lovely young woman and first-time dog owner. Samantha came to me because she was discouraged by her dog's behaviour. George was destroying her house and would turn walks into physical battles. Samantha was angry and on the verge of surrendering George. I could see that the bond between them was disrupted and dysfunctional. I immediately proposed we begin a SCAT program to move things along quickly and effortlessly.

Training started during that very first visit. I asked Samantha why she was angry, and what did she fear losing. Her answer was typical: she was angry that George was breaking her possessions and being hyper-reactive in public. I followed with the fear questions. Samantha answered she was afraid of losing her social status, reputation, and self-worth.

Those were deep-rooted emotions emanating from her ego. We sat with George and I asked her to look at him and tell me what she saw in him as bad and what she could enumerate as good. Samantha told me he was not a good dog, that his behaviour was out of control, that he was impatient, and that he never listened to her. The positive answers characterized him as loving, very athletic, a fast learner, and as having endless curiosity and determination. I told Samantha to reclaim those ideas as her own. She acknowledged my proposal and started to enumerate how those ideas applied to her life. I wrote her answers and revelations in her file.

Samantha was an overachiever who had inconsistent caregivers/owners. Her "mother" would enable her inappropriate behaviour, while her "father" took a dictatorial approach to her upbringing. The behaviour we observed in George was indeed a reflection of Samantha's inner workings. Her ego was screaming injustice, which was a cover-up for the fear of losing her identity. Extrapolating further: ego is your identity and associates with the body, and death of body equates with death of ego. Ego does not want the body to die, yet ego is slowly trying to kill the body. The vicious body-death-ego-death cycle creates a state of mind which prevents normal perception, and Samantha was certainly not alone in experiencing the emotional turmoil of ego. Fear of death is the number one negative emotion driven by the mental torment of the ego.

The next step in our process was to test Samantha's attachment style with George. I use Ainsworth's (1969) strange-situation test to determine attachment types. The process is very simple. I asked Samantha to bring the dog into the next room. There, my assistant would enter, engage with George and the owner. Samantha would then leave. My assistant would interact with George to determine his behaviours and attachment style. Finally, Samantha would return and interact with George as my assistant left the room. I could observe the scene from the other room via a camera. I determined that George had an ambivalent attachment towards Samantha. Ambivalence and inconsistency go hand in hand.

Her first series of cognitive exercise were two rounds of Brain Games. The first series was a beginner level game made with recyclable materials. The second round of games was an intermediate level. I use commercial games to increase the level of difficulty, as it is easier to document progress this way. We followed up with a training exercise called "Check-in." Social learning encourages the dog to make the proper decision or auto-correct its choice to suit the request.

In other words, I would wait for George to look at Samantha before I would reinforce the check-in behaviour. We do not ask for the behaviour or give a cue; we simply wait for the dog to make the right choice. The process takes a little longer, but our goal is not to change behaviour. Rather, our goal is to teach George to learn how to learn, to effectively problem-solve and auto-correct his own behaviour.

My overall objective is to create a functional human-animal bond between Samantha and George, which, in turn, increases their ability to self-regulate. If Samantha can change her behaviour through George, and George modifies his behaviour through Samantha, their human-dog bond reflects the perfect symbiotic relationship. I made a circular model that looks something like the following image (Figure 11). The small oval, which joins the two human/dog aggression circles, is where we would place the figurative mirror to stop the projection. I picked aggression as an example, but you can place any emotion within the model.

One might think dogs do not need mental exercises because they are not very smart. Although it seems that way, dogs like George are normally very smart, and science is on a mission to prove just how smart they really are. I often refer to the structure of a dog brain as a 2.5-year-old high-functioning autistic child. My definition might shock, but please read on. Dogs are extremely intelligent, but their small frontal lobes and their oversize limbic systems let emotion overrule cognition. Cognitive exercises allow us to sort out emotions and access learning abilities. Think of a funnel: the large opening represents emotions and the small opening is cognition. Once we reduce the emotional output, we can access cognition, more specifically, learning abilities. Our objective with George was to centre his attention on one specific task.

Cognition can be a challenge for dogs like George because emotions are on overdrive, especially during dog adolescence. We cannot access the mind when emotions occur above threshold and when resilience is poor. When those two criteria are present, we need another set of tools to help humans and non-humans to bypass their emotions and access learning. This is where the social determinant intervenes. George, the overly enthusiastic adolescent dog, is so eager to work that he would jump out of his skin if he could. George often becomes a danger to himself when he is overexcited. Therefore, the first training exercise I demonstrated to Samantha was a physical contention.

A contention is an impulse-control containment strategy, which occurs when we gently compress the dog with our arms. I compress the dog against my body with sufficient tension to hold him in place. Note I did not say "squeeze," for I am not confining the dog, I am simply holding him. I immediately release the compression when the dog relaxes. I repeat this pressure-on-pressure-off procedure until I can release the dog and he does not bolt out of my arms. I finally give the release command when he calmly looks at me. The dog should quickly shake off and return to normal.

I teach my clients how to master this procedure. Temple Grandin (2005) talks about physical contention in her book entitled *Animals in Translation: Using the Mysteries of Autism to Decode Animal Behaviour*. In her book, she describes how she designed a *squeeze machine* for herself when emotions became overwhelming. "When I saw the cattle in their squeeze chute and got inspired to build a squeeze machine for myself, at first I was thinking only about the calming effects of deep pressure." (Grandin, 2005, p. 114). She explains how she subsequently added padding and experienced new sensations and feelings like *gentleness* and *kindness*, which overall made her feel more socially adjusted and calm.

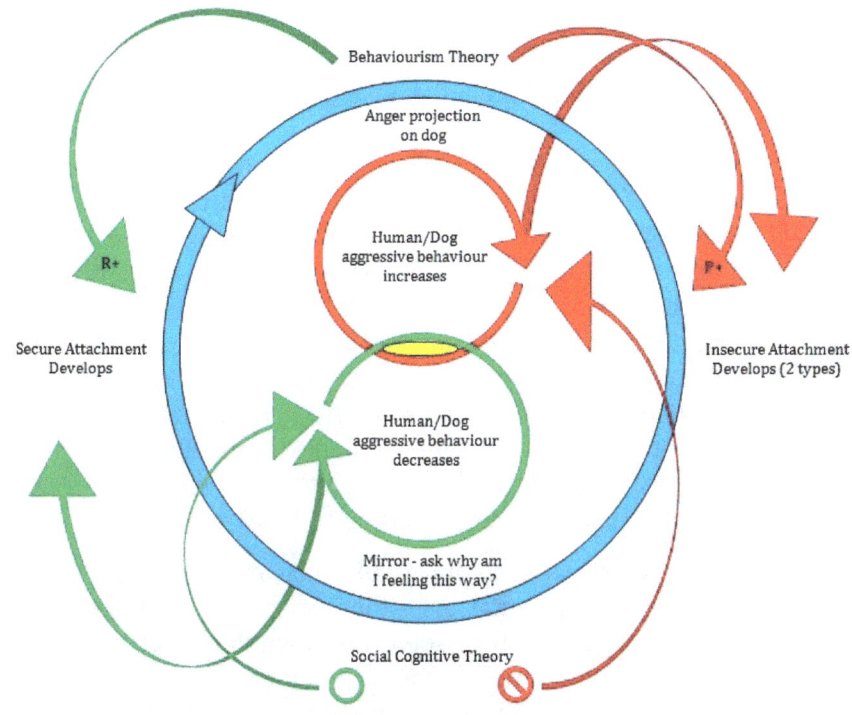

Figure 11. The human-dog bond.

The following social exercises were easier and less invasive. The first exercise would require Samantha to massage George in specific areas using soft and continuous strokes and by making eye contact as often as possible. Finally, Samantha would lie with George on the floor for approximately 5 minutes. Social contact, without petting, is very reinforcing for dogs. Constantly stroking dogs, on the other hand, can become overstimulating very quickly. We have a rule when we interact with animals, especially wolves, we pet or scratch only for 5 to 10 seconds at a time, and stop. If the animal leans in or changes sides and looks at you with soft eyes, we resume the caress for another 5 to 10 seconds. But if the animal freezes or moves away, the social interaction is over. Cat owners know this rule without being conscious of it. When feline caregivers pet their cat, especially on its belly, people quickly learn that the 0 to 100 reaction time occurs in 0.001 seconds. Cats tolerate petting until they clearly do not.

The first imitation exercise I gave Samantha was yawning. I invited Samantha to sit on the floor, at eye level with George, and perform the most convincing yawn she could. George had 90 seconds to respond with a yawn. George yawned at 87 seconds. We repeated the exercise 5 times, and George got faster after each repetition. The following exercise was, and still is my favourite game. I instructed Samantha to sit in the chair. We were going to talk for a few minutes, and unexpectedly, she would display the most convincing stretch she could, without looking at George or me. George would again have 90 seconds to stretch. The stretch exercise is harder because it includes a series of behaviours: attention, stand, stretch front, and stretch back. Sometimes dogs add a yawn to the stretch, and in this case, we ignored yawn.

Imitation is a complex rule to learn; however, when a human-dog team masters the learning strategy, new possibilities manifest themselves. Samantha was curious about imitation and inquired what it entailed. I explained how imitation allows us to train complex behaviours in a fraction of time; however, we first had to train three behaviours on verbal cue (Fugazza, 2014; Fugazza & Miklósi, 2015). Since there are no negative consequences to the imitation training process, we agreed on the behaviours we would train to teach the rule of imitation and started the process.

I proposed we work towards the imitation rule and prepare for a worst-case scenario. During the process, George would have fun learning new behaviours. The worst-case scenario meant that George would be unable to learn imitation and the rule would become useless. Samantha agreed it could satisfy George's incessant desire to learn. George barked, and we laughed.

To start the training plan, we needed to identify which behaviours Samantha wanted to address first. She told me her deepest desire was to accept herself and George as *perfectly imperfect*. Samantha was adamant about relinquishing her yearning to accomplish everything as fast and as perfectly as possible, all the time. Therefore, as a first target behaviour we chose surrendering the ego.

If you know me, you know that I call an elephant an elephant, and clients soon learn one thing from SCAT: the ego does not like it when I point out the elephant, so to speak. Like a child on a wild tantrum, the ego does not abdicate easily. The first exercise I gave Samantha was a *release-after-event* response: when George made her angry, I asked Samantha to forgive him as soon as possible after the event and document her timing. It took a little more than a day for Samantha to get over her own anger during their first human-dog conflict. Unfortunately, Samantha's mind took off at lightning speed and she found it difficult to release her thoughts and forgive herself. However, her response time did increase throughout the following months.

The following exercise I gave Samantha was the *calm* behaviour. The exercise consists of combining muscle relaxation with breathing. Breathing exercises are also known as pranayama, the Sanskrit word for *life force extension*. This behaviour is relatively simple to train when you know how to accomplish it through imitation. When the dog gets excited, sit on the ground and start to breathe in Nadhi (alternate nostril breathing) or Ujjayi (ocean breath). Although both techniques serve to calm the mind, Nadhi tends to cool the body and Ujjayi to warm it. The specific exercise I gave Samantha was a Nadhi three-step breath with retention on the exhale, which mimics deep-sleep breathing in dogs.

The following is the first exercise I give most of my clients and students. You can practice it as you read along. Sit comfortably, relax all your body parts, and clear your nose and throat. Fold your fingers, as demonstrated in Figure 12, and start the following sequence.

- Place your right thumb on your right nostril, and close it. Keep it closed.

- Inhale through the left nostril for 6 seconds.

- Close your left nostril with your pinkie and ring finger.

- Hold your breath for 4 seconds.

- Release your thumb on the right side and exhale for 6 seconds.

- Close the right side and hold for 4 seconds.

- Repeat the same process on the other side.

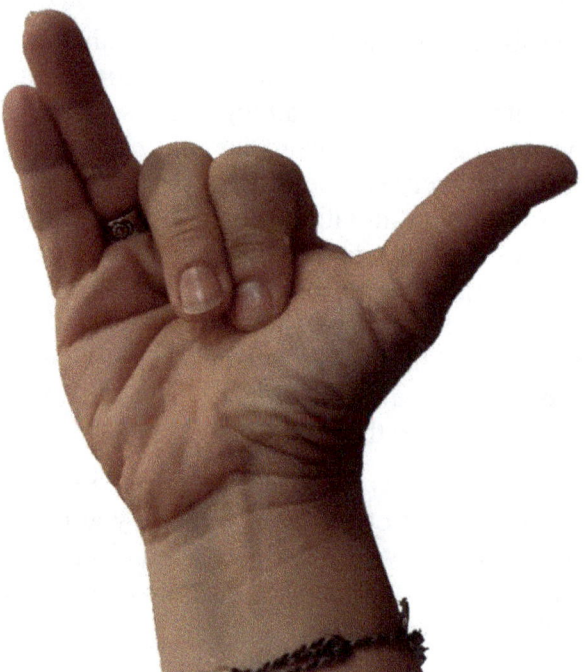

Figure 12. Nadhi fingers.

The goal of the exercise is to increase the exhalation and extend its length without straining your respiration. Do not worry if you cannot accomplish the pranayama at this time. Breathing is an exercise that requires practice. On the other hand, your dog should recognize this pattern as peaceful and start to relax as soon as you change your breathing rhythm. The wonderful thing about imitation is that you can apply the technique to various aspects of your inter-species relationship. Imitation not only serves behaviour but applies to emotions.

We are fortunate to share a left gaze bias with dogs, and vice versa (Guo et al., 2009). Remember, we read emotions by scanning facial features from the left to the right, which in reality is the opposite side of the face. In other words, we decode emotions on the left side of the dog's face. Every dog has an asymmetrical face that slants on the left side. If you do not believe me, look at the left side of the face of the dog closest to you: you will immediately see a difference in the eyes. The older the dog is, the more prevalent the features will be.

Look at the images of Albear below (Figure 13). The top left image, his face is neutral as I take the picture. The top right image shows him as I smiled while taking the photo. The bottom left photo shows the left side of his face cut, flipped, and pasted together. The bottom right image is the right side of his face cut, flipped, and pasted together. Do you see a change? If so, what has changed? I will give you a clue. Look at his eyes and ears. The top right photo clearly shows his left eye slightly closed as I smiled at him. Albear was emotionally responding to my smile as I snapped the image. Again, try it with your dogs, take a photo head-on, observe their features, and note the variations.

We can use this information to communicate more effectively with our dogs, and we can influence our dog's emotions when we consciously modify our internal discourse. Social-cognitive learning is a natural process we can nourish intentionally. For Samantha, the emotional left gaze bias was a revelation. She learned how to tap into George's emotions by acknowledging the negative reactions, changing her responses to them, and projecting a new positive outcome within herSelf and George. I call that efficient and effective training.

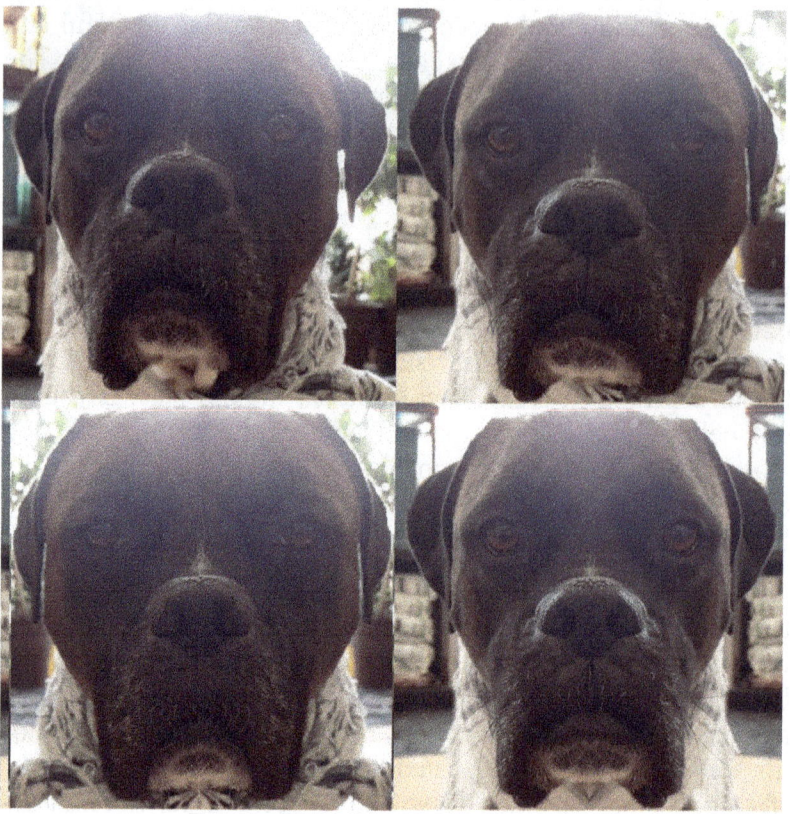

Figure 13. Albear, left gaze bias.

The SCAT process in a nutshell

The SCAT process (Figure 14) might seem complex because science and spirituality are not normally seen as being related and in harmony. Yet, the simplicity of the system transcends sensory perception and raises the human experience to the ultimate experience of truth: the natural human experience of love. Furthermore, the multifaceted approach addresses and facilitates our spiritual journey. With the help of our canine companions, we can deal with fear and anger at the quantum level.

In the process of behaviour modification and spiritual growth, you might wonder if dogs have a spiritual life; unfortunately, science cannot answer that question, at least not yet. My response would be that *it does not matter*. For dogs are part of the illusion that we are separate from the universal energy, nothing more, nothing less. Does it mean we should neglect, abuse, or stop caring for them? Obviously not! Our responsibility, while we are in the illusion, is to experience life as the sum total of positive outcomes to our loving actions; and in my opinion, that includes dogs.

My experience with SCAT over the last 13 years has been a marvellous voyage, inside and out. I work with social-cognitive learning, study the science behind cognitive-neuroscience, and train my dog by applying the theory. I recently revised and modified the triangular model to incorporate attachment and spirituality. In the proposed version (see Figure 14), the unity field connects all human and non-human organisms at the quantum level. Each living entity interacts and affects the experiences of every other entity. When a direction is interrupted or broken, the system falls apart, and positive experiences become negative.

The SCAT model strives to reconcile all determinants through extension instead of projection. Remember: extension is love directed outwardly and serves to uplift others; projection is ego propelled outwardly and serves to repress others.

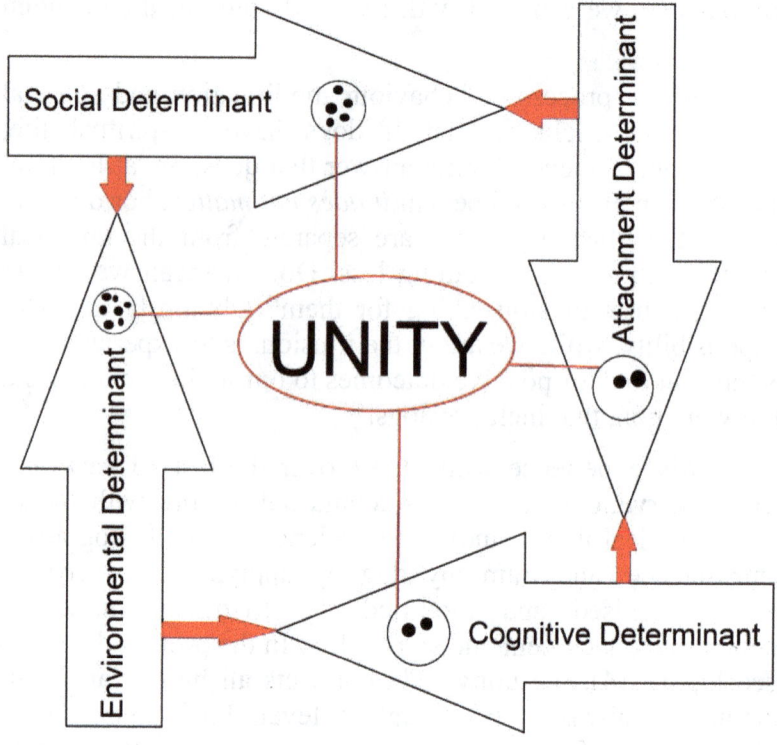

Figure 14. Social-cognitive attachment training (SCAT).

Case study: Albear

The last case study is my own. If you have met my dog Albear, you probably recognize the SCAT model at work, for I raised and trained Albear using this scientific/spiritual approach, as I like to call it. I adopted Albear when he was 7 weeks old. My son and I were to foster a puppy that was born in a small storage unit. Someone abandoned the pregnant female at the establishment the night before Albear was born; thankfully, Albear the puppy found his way to our home, and we embarked on the fostering adventure. A series of events occurred that quickly changed our lives.

Three days after Albear's arrival, we returned home after work to a burning building. My house was on fire and we had no more home. Albear experienced the ordeal as if it was all just part of a normal day. I saw his facial expression and knew, at that moment—while fire trucks, police officers, and ambulances were hard at work battling the blaze and saving lives—that Albear would never leave my care. When our lives returned to normal, I started to train Albear with the SCAT model.

On my way to work, a week after the fire, I placed Albear in a socio-cognitive exercise and he took it from there. Albear is not a particularly smart dog. I have never lied or tried to fool myself about his intellect. What makes Albear special is his desire to think outside the box. My dog has an endless desire to try new things because he knows our relationship gets stronger with each attempt he makes. With each new improvisation or behavioural auto-correction, Albear has always done his very best. At 5 years old, Albear discovered, on his own, that human laughter is reinforcing. I still remember the day he developed a sense of humour.

The second event that changed our lives occurred when Albear was a year and a half old. We were returning from a walk when we were both surprised by a bagpipe and drum practice in the park across the street. The sound frightened me and traumatized Albear. I knew we could not leave, not with fear coursing through our bodies. I did cognitive exercises with him until he felt a little more comfortable. We left when Albear looked at me and shook. When, at nearly 8 years-old, Albear hears drums or bagpipes, he asks for my help, and each time I offer it because our relationship is a reflection of my own spiritual journey. We will never stop working at this because SCAT is more than a dog-training model; it is a way of life, a philosophy if you will.

The perfect recipe for raising the perfect puppy does not exist; but if it did, SCAT would surely be it. First, learn dog language; second, take a 7-week old puppy and socialize him appropriately and adequately, practice social-cognitive exercises, train with reinforcement, expose to novelty, bond, name stimuli, become attached (but not emotionally dependent), relax, breath, and release ego. Your dog does not need a fancy car, condominium, clothing, furniture, or travel purse. Your dog needs you, the human being not the human doing, hiding behind all those layers of artificial illusions. Take some time to be with your dog and enjoy life as an experience, not as a challenge. No one wins the game of life; we all end at game-over time.

So make the journey fun and colourful. I do not consider Albear to be *my* dog, for that would mean that I possessed him, making the ego real. *"My whatever"* renders the illusion factual and nourishes fear. To believe in possessions is to reinforce the dream. I prefer to acknowledge Albear as a unique expression of universal energy. I share my life with him, and one day, he will die. When the time comes, Albear will return to the universal energy, and I will have no choice but to consider *my dog* as *a dog*, for at the quantum level, the dog is god.

In the meantime, Albear rewards me each day with his comical and debonair attitude. He has had many outfits over the years, yet the one that describes him most accurately is a pipe smoking university professor nestled in a comfortable leather armchair at the library, with his French beret tilted to the side, reading the latest quantum physics cartoon strip. If Albear had a part in Big Bang Theory, he would be Sheldon's mischievous joke, a sort of Forrest Gump sidekick. He would not know how he became a physicist, but he would succeed because he is one with the universal energy. The most amazing thing about dogs is their ability to live life without ego, hence, without a distorted perspective. So why not enjoy their pure creative potential and laugh a little?

Social-cognitive attachment training serves to unite animals and humans in order to facilitate human enlightenment. Dogs are preeminent teachers, who help modify our perception and make the transition from ego to god. Once we recognize dogs teach us important spiritual lessons, we can actively change our awareness from a negative to a positive life experience by simply choosing to. Free will is our superpower. When human perception shifts, dog behaviour improves. When people replace fear with love, projection turns into extension:

in other words, a miracle. To the ultimate separation problem, only one solution exists, forgiveness. With the help of dogs, science reunites man with god, for it is in unity that we find the peace of god.

The entire human experience is in need of rectification, and dogs are our strongest allies when it comes to correcting our perceptions. Once the ego changes direction and gets "off track" as it were, the secure attachment and symbiotic relationship we experience with our dogs immediately dissolves and the dogs project back, becoming restless, frustrated, impatient, defensive, and disobedient. We can acknowledge the process and change our perceptions by releasing fear. From there, extension increases because the thought of separation no longer drives behaviour. Unity affects not only human behaviour but inadvertently modifies dog behaviour. When we reunite with the universal energy of love, dogs experience relaxation, joy, patience, and friendship.

At the end of the day, the true human experience is about reconnecting with one another. Every single human on earth shares the same purpose. The hole we seek to fill, the void we wish to satisfy, and the emptiness we want to appease, all serve to re-mind us of our true identity as expressions of the universal energy; ergo, the essence of humanity is to share our loving function with others. People are not destined to fear, much less fight with each other. We know that negative such feelings and actions are detrimental to our existence. So why do people insist on destroying their brothers and sisters? The answer is our ego has a grasp on our mind and believes that separation is true.

I end this chapter with a surrender ego exercise: the best way to reconnect with the universal energy is to meditate and recite a Mantra or Sutra. Although Sutras are scriptures, some people recite them as Mantras. The choice is yours. While you meditate, repeat a Mantra or Sutra that defines you as a universal energy particle. My favourite Mantra, as you might have guessed, is OM.

Decisions are continuous. You do not always know when you are making them. But with a little practice with the ones you recognise, a set begins to form which sees you through the rest. (ACIM, 2007, T-30.I.1:1)

Reader notes

Chapter 8: Dog in the Mirror is God

Energy summary

I would like to summarize the previous chapters into a shorter one, followed by one sentence and a one-word summary. Each review that follows corresponds directly to its chapter title. The reason behind the structure is to allow for repetition and accessibility for future reference. First, repetition is necessary to create new habits. I repeated concepts, ideas, rules, and protocols because behaviour changes are difficult to modify, especially in humans. Without repetition, we forget what we are doing or why. I hope that the concepts elaborated in the previous chapters have become deeply embedded in your mind, and that you now have a basic knowledge and understanding of the scientific/spiritual approach I presented to you. If you still struggle to understand, then this section becomes important, so I will present the summaries again.

Should you wish to revisit certain sections of this book, you can come to this section and consult which chapter corresponds to the information you seek. The sentence and word summary can help you remember the basic idea behind each chapter. I have added a few lines in case you wish to write your personal thoughts in this section. Do not be afraid to explore your inner world. Spirit is full of creative potential that can benefit others, since each person is an expression of god, of the universal energy. Share your inner workings; you might be surprised by the outcome.

You can apply the following summary model to your event recollection when you analyze past projections and wish to unearth the emotion associated with the conflict. With time, you will be able to apply this model immediately, in order to access the negative emotion. Tech savvy people can record their recollection of the conflict immediately after the event and fill out a summary. I have used both techniques in the past, and they work wonderfully. Who knows, someone might develop an app for that.

Universal energy keeps all matter and living things united at the quantum level. Each level of matter builds upon itself and entanglement preserves unity by never altering the connection that binds particles together. Einstein thought the proxy, aka spin, could be found in the particle (Isaacson, 2008; Folger, 2004; Lewis & Veritasium, 2015); I tend to agree with science that the proxy is not *in* the particle, but rather *is* the particle. I believe science will one day demonstrate that spin is the actual bonding agent of a particle. As with spirituality, god is not in you; god is you. You can never solely affect one particle, one cell, one person without affecting another. The balance of the universe depends on dichotomies, for without a positive to a negative or a negative to a positive, there is nothing, yet there is everything.

Universal energy includes opposites, which eliminates separation. One could say unity includes itself. The connection between other people and our dogs is inseparable by space or time. If quantum physics binds us at the infinitely small level of the particle, empathy links dogs and people at the infinitely large physical level.

One sentence summary: The energy source can never be separate.
One word summary: Unity

_____
_____
_____
_____

Emotion summary

The brain is a complex system that controls a giant machine. The cerebrum controls a great deal of information in a very short amount of time; consequently, the brain works extremely hard when you interact with other living organisms that influence who you are and you become each passing moment. The mind and body form a partnership during adolescence, and ego takes control of the body. When the ego, mind, body trinity controls your experience of the world, projection starts. Memories form and experiences modify our behaviours.

In essence, we become the sum of other people's actions. Science is still searching to locate mirror neurons; until then, imitation seems to confirm that we connect through an emotional system. I believe the system in question is empathy. We know emotions are contagious and modify behaviour; in turn, both human and non-human actions influence each other. If we did not connect emotionally, we could not influence each other. Spiritually, we strive to decondition ego and its grasp on our biology to release fear and access our true function: forgiveness and love. We can change the mind-thought system if we accept that reality is an illusion. The process is difficult but not impossible.

One sentence summary: Ego controls biology and experiences through sensory organs.
One word summary: Function

_____
_____
_____
_____

Behaviour summary

Projection functions as a defence mechanism created by the ego to protect itself and the body against perceived external threats and dangers. Perception is an extremely powerful tool created by our senses, which often leads to misinterpretation. Conversely, the ego distorts perceptions because it, too, seeks self-destruction. With ego, there is no balance: extremes rule and create fear, which in turn, feed the illusion by confirming that the world is dangerous and scary. The images we perceive are sometimes horrific, yet they are unreal.

Furthermore, learning theories such as behaviourism and social-cognitivism forge our behaviour through conditioning and empathic learning. When conditioning is positive, our mind perceives experiences as pleasant. Conversely, if learning is negative, the ego perceives experiences as unpleasant. In either case, the result is still a faulty perception that leads to undesirable behaviour. We can stop the projection with meditation and other relaxing practices. Introspection calms the ego and allows people to reconnect with the universal energy. Dogs are our spiritual partners, for they show us our projections without judgement. Humans benefit from the symbiotic relationship because ego manifests through an unbiased filter, which we can further acknowledge and release.

One sentence summary: The ego experiences separation because projection creates perception.
One word summary: Fear

_____
_____
_____
_____

Unity summary

To mirror is to reflect back; consequently, the mirroring process serves to recognize faulty behaviour in our dogs as reflections of our own inadequacies and inner mind-thought processes. When you look deeply within yourSelf, you realize two things: you are not a body and the ego no longer serves a purpose. Once you understand the effects of mirroring, there is no turning back. Ego becomes an autopilot that keeps you safe without your needing to think cognitively; thus, the mind is free to express its true loving nature and help heal others. You will then look at the world and your dog without faulty perceptions. Human and dog symbiotic relationships will serve a new function as forgiveness enhances your experiences. Love will extend outwards and nourish the collective unconscious.

As people awaken from the dream, their creative potential will emanate from a collective mind and allow the thought process to enhance the physical experience without judgment or guilt. The fear of death will become obsolete because there will no longer be a need to identify with the physical. The body will regain its original function as a vessel for the spirit. Interactions will serve to awaken people to the reality that biological life is simply an illusion.

One sentence summary: Ego no longer controls the mind and releases its creative potential.
One word summary: Forgiveness

_____
_____
_____
_____

Social-cognitive summary

Once projection ceases to share destructive ideas, the mechanism that influences the thought of separation and negative emotions comes to a halt. With social-cognitive learning, we can train our minds to perceive new meaning in environments that were once destructive. As people, we constantly need to live in the present moment in order to assess the social, cognitive, and environmental determinants, for their influence insidiously alters behaviour.

The bi-directional model includes the human and dog as a morphic unit. The reciprocal determinism system changes direction when we achieve forgiveness. Ideas of unity fill the mind, regardless of the environment, and emotions of love unite individuals at the fundamental core.

Universal energy, like an electric current, requires a proper alignment to function. When the corrected mind communicates with the body, the feeling of emptiness disappears, separation turns to unification, and darkness leads to light. Insecure attachments transform into secure feelings of connectedness; consequently, morphic fields expand outwards, sharing positive energy, which in turn, feed the collective unit. As spirit forgives ego, the corrected mind releases negative energy, and the body finally heals.

One sentence summary: The adjusted mind transforms the body from disease to ease.
One word summary: Correction

_____
_____
_____
_____

Big picture summary

Social-cognitive attachment training is a training model designed to include all learning theories into one general method. The SCAT process extrapolates on Cimarelli, Turcsán, Range, and Virányi (2017) who tested the idea that securely attached dogs respond and react to social threats better than insecurely attached pairs. When we train to change an insecure attachment to a secure one, not only do we modify behaviour, we transform emotions at their core. SCAT protocols deepen relationships and open entirely new levels of learning for both dogs and humans alike.

The most amazing phenomena regarding social-cognitive training is behaviour problems disappear as you awaken to a new reality. The reason you have a dog will also change. No longer seen as an object or possession, dogs will take on the role of human healer. Other possessions will also appear less desirable, for the need to fill the emptiness will disappear. Love is the construct behind universal energy, and through acceptance and forgiveness, love as a mechanism only serves to extend. Love does not have levels or degrees, and SCAT serves to extend the universal energy that binds us together.

One sentence summary: Interspecies exchange that offers a bidirectional healing strategy.
One word summary: Transformation

A Scientific/spiritual summary

To take multiple approaches and combine them into one functional system requires a global view not only of humans, but also of non-human animals, society, the world and the universe. It requires an understanding of how the infinitely small and immensely large function together. Science likes to segment and the brain constantly tries to generalize. The dichotomy represents yet another level of confusion. Life is a constant representation of the inescapable truth: the ego believes in separation. We have discussed various solutions to end separation, yet there is one more thing remaining to state: change will not occur overnight. Neither SCAT, nor any other strategy, can claim to cure a mind that does not know it is ill. No pill exists that can waken you from a dream, if you do not know you are sleeping in the first place.

The enlightenment, i.e., the awakening process can be understood using the following analogy: imagine you are in a pitch-black room with a door and a light interrupter. At the bottom of the door, there is an infinitely faint ray of light coming through. Ego is in a dark room and moves around feeling and perceiving its way towards the interrupter. Every now and then, ego perceives the light, but the luminosity is simply not strong enough to serve as a guide. Suddenly, another being turns on a very soft light source that helps you move more easily. Together you approach the door, for the light interrupter would only serve to illuminate the room. Your guide knows the room is not real; consequently, spirit strives to show you reality, that there is life beyond the room, beyond the container. Until you can see the light, you have to trust the spirit. You have to believe that the spirit guides you towards a better reality, away from illusion and far from projection.

Remember, projection creates perception, for there is nothing to see, hear, touch, smell, or speak when you are in the dark. Senses mean nothing to the spirit. The ego, however, needs to fill in the black, so it invents its own reality. At the same time, spirit seeks to guide you towards the door with a dimmer light source. It could bring you closer to the door, but just like your biological eyes, you cannot expose an untrained mind to its source, for you would create resistance.

Have you ever tried to turn on a light in the middle of the night, only to have your physical eyes immediately close because of the pain of the bright light? The same happens to the ego; hence, the reason why the process takes time. However, once you softly and slowly open your metaphysical eyes and let them adjust, you will find your way out of the room much more quickly and, eventually, reach the door and connect with the universal energy. Unfortunately, all one can do is offer guidance towards the light; inevitably, it is the responsibility of the guided to walk through the door and join the metaphysical sunshine. There are challenges along the way that make the process seem overwhelming. But rest assured, you will advance faster than you anticipated; for once an awakened mind is exposed to the truth, it can no longer un-know.

I propose that we conduct one last exercise: you will need a comfortable chair, silence, and a window. Sit quietly in the chair with your legs comfortably bent, your back fully supported, your arms resting on the armrest or legs; then look towards the window. The exercise is similar to the one proposed in **Step 3 - Forgive Conflict** above. Take three deep breaths while you focus on your thoughts without judgment.

When you exhale, imagine you release your ideas outward. Once you are done, remain in the same position and start to visualize the empty space you feel within yourself. When you reach the feeling of anxiety fuelled by fear, imagine there is a love bubble filled with light and universal knowledge. Step into the bubble and let your mind-body connection fade away. Know that you are one hundred percent safe and loved.

There is no judgment here and no fear. Peace and abundance surround you. Ego will try to befuddle the mind; however, simply experience the distraction and return to the fullness. You should feel as if a warm presence is embracing you. The feeling is similar to when a person places a warm towel on your arms and back for comfort. There is no better spiritual sensation than the experience of being human. Now, open your eyes very slowly and experience the pain and adjustment. Note how much time it took for your eyes to readjust to colour and light. The meditation serves to release fear and realign the ego, mind, and body triad to its original function as universal energy, egregor, and spirit trinity. Although the process might seem to take forever, spirit time does not exist; thus, the idea of separation was resolved the moment it occurred.

One sentence summary: Expansion and collapse of universal energy is the breath of god.
One word summary: Love

_____
_____
_____
_____

> *"People like us, who believe in physics, know that distinction made between past, present and future is nothing more than a persistent, stubborn illusion."* — Albert Einstein

Final thoughts

A thought comes to mind as I write the final sentences of this book. What would happen if every single person who read this book told someone they know: *I'm afraid of...* My guess is that people would start to reassure each other, and relationships would deepen because family, friends, or colleagues would nourish love. Morphic fields would expand with a very positive energy and spread to other fields. Morphic resonance would further expand love because the imprint humans would have on one another would share the memory of unity, not separation.

I know it might sound utopian to think we can change behaviour through acceptance and the acknowledgement that we are all afraid of the same thing. But I deeply believe that we have no choice but to do so. The time has come for us to see our dogs as expressions of ourselves, whether we like what we see or not, and reevaluate our projections, perceptions, behaviours, and thoughts when necessary.

We need to plumb the depths of universal energy and allocate love to those who are still overwhelmed and angry at the world they have come to believe is the enemy. We now know the true enemy is the ego, and the only way to appease the destructive inner chatter is to forgive the confused mind and replace fear with love. The power of a positive approach far exceeds the most negative destructive force one can imagine. My friend and long-departed training partner used to say *power is in numbers*; in other words, when we unite we can move mountains: literally, figuratively, and metaphysically. Too many humans have lost their sense of direction and belonging, and too many of us watch on as they fade away.

Unity is our guiding force, for the collective creative potential overcomes adversity. Once people accept and cherish their function, extension will naturally occur. People and dogs in my immediate surrounding are my true inspiration, for we all navigate through the intricacies of life, wondering what the next chapter of our adventures will yield. As we come up with original solutions to our problems, I can only rejoice in the fact that dogs do not care if we are too this or too that. Our canine companions simply care about the present moment and how we can come together, as different species, and cherish the experiences life sends our way. One thing I have learned from my dogs is to take it all in with a big dollop of humour.

Those of you who know me will recall my passion for making reference to song lyrics, movie, and television quotes. I cannot end my first book without mentioning that I have added bits of humour in many passages of this book. So to those who are unfamiliar with my humorous side, I say *"To infinity, and beyond!"* And for the Star Wars generations who recall the sentence *"May the force be with you,"* my wish for you is to have a clearer and deeper understanding of what that actually signifies. I could go on, but I will spare you my comedy.

Thus, as my time with you ends, I can honestly say that writing this book has been a most enriching adventure. Don't get me wrong! my life journey has been a splendidly interesting and fabulous adventure, worthy of a Jumanji sequel. Who knows, maybe one day I will share it with you. In the meantime, I hope I was able to give you a strong enough nudge to awaken your spiritual voice and allow it to guide you and your dog towards symbiosis.

I know firsthand how difficult certain life challenges can be and how hard it is to change perceptions, so my heart goes out to you as you and your dog embark on the enlightenment journey. Know that my morphic field reaches outward to supports yours, and never forget that what you do to others, you are in fact doing to yourself. It sounds like a cliché, but it is the truth.

When you think about it, prayers are truly requests made on behalf of yourSelf for yourself. Prayers never give you what you want and invocations only send what you need. For how can god give if the ego refuses to receive? It is a subtle distinction and a powerful revelation. True requests come from spirit and serve to awaken the ego, and once the mind shifts, miracles can happen. As Mahatma Gandhi said, "Be the change you want to see in the world."

Thirty years ago, I wanted to change the world. I did not know how, but I was determined to find out. I set out to include humans and dogs in the process because of our mutual fondness. One dog changed my life, and I am grateful beyond words for Boreal's patience. She taught me many life lessons; but most importantly, she taught me to change myself, if I was going to ask her to change.

Today, I know I cannot change the world, but I can, and have, modified my perception of it. And from there, I see the world transform right before my eyes. Dogs did not join us because we made them. Dogs became our allies because we share a common goal. The unity between humans and dogs is based on one irrefutable truth: forgiveness. My dog forgives me for my lack of canine abilities, and I forgive my dog for his lack of human abilities. If you retain only one message from this book, let it be: *ultimately, it doesn't matter if we lack, for we love.*

What are awesome final words and thoughts you ask? To be honest, I have been asking mySelf that exact questions. How does one end a book that discusses universal energy, quantum physics, human behaviour, dog training, and spirituality? First, I decided to use a famous quote. Then I thought to include a passage from my favourite book. But neither of these felt authentic. So I procrastinated. Finally, it came to me during meditation: if I am to stay true to mySelf, to you, and to my dog, the only words I can express without compromising the entire integrity of this manuscript is: I love you.

If they stand above you, watch them.
If they stand behind you, protect them.
If they stand beside you, respect them.
If they stand against you, love them.

Reader' notes

References

Abrantes, R. (1997a). *Dog Language, An Encyclopaedia of Canine Behaviour*. Naperville, IL: Wakan Tanka Publishers.

———. (1997b). *The Evolution of Canine Social Behaviour*. Naperville, IL: Wakan Tanka Publishers.

Ainsworth, M. S. (1979). Infant-mother attachment. *American Psychologist*, Vol. 34, No. 10, pp. 932-937. DOI: 10.1037/0003-066X.34.10.932

Ainsworth, M. S. & Witting, B.A. (1969). Attachment and the exploratory behaviour of one-year-olds in a strange situation. *Determinants of Infant Behaviour*, Vol. 4, No. 4, pp. 113-136. DOI: n/a.

Aldred, C. (1991). *Akhenaten: King of Egypt*. London, United Kingdom: Thames & Hudson.

Amoss, M. S. Jr. & Hodges, C. M. (1995). Selected Parameters of the Reproductive Physiology and Endocrinology of Coyotes. University of Nebraska - Lincoln, USA. *Symposium Proceedings - Coyotes in the Southwest: A Compendium of Our Knowledge*, paper 44.

Arnold, D. (n.d.). *Madhyamaka Buddhist Philosophy*. Internet Encyclopaedia of Philosophy. Retrieved from http://www.iep.utm.edu/b-madhya/#H2 November 2017

Arntz, W. (Producer) and Arntz, W., Chasse, B. & Vicente, M. (Director). (2004). *What The Bleep Do We Know!?* Film from Roadside Attractions. 197min.

———. (2014). *What the Bleep Do We Know?!* [Educational DVD]

Arntz, W., Chasse, B. & Vincente, M. (2006). *What The Bleep Do We Know!?* Deerfield Beach, Florida: Health Communication.

Awareness Act. (2017). "Spirituality Without Quantum Physics Is an Incomplete Picture of Reality, According to the Dalai Lama." 17 November. Retrieved from http://awarenessact.com/spirituality-without-quantum-physics-is-an-incomplete-picture-of-reality-according-to-the-dalai-lama/?=AA

Bandura, A. (1965). Influence of models' reinforcement contingencies on the acquisition of imitative responses. *Journal of Personality and Social Psychology*, Vol. 1, No. 6, pp. 589-595. DOI: 10.1037/h0022070

———. (1977). Self-efficacy: Toward a unifying theory of behavioural change. *Psychological Review*, Vol. 84, No. 2, pp. 191-215. DOI: 10.1037/0033-295X.84.2.191

———. (1989). Social cognitive theory. In R. Vasta (Ed.). *Annals of child development. Vol. 6. Six theories of child development* (pp. 1-60). Greenwich, CT: JAI Press

———. (2001). Social Cognitive Theory: An Agentic Perspective. *Annual Review of Psychology*, Vol. 52, No. 1, pp. 1-60. DOI: 10.1146/annurev.psych.52.1.1

Beebe, S., Beebe, S., Redmon, M. & Geerinck, T. (2007). *Interpersonal Communication*. Toronto, Ontario: Pearson Education Canada.

Bekoff, M. (2007). *The Emotional Lives of Animals*. Novato, CA: New World Library.

Bekoff, M. & Gese, E. M. (2003). Coyote (Canis latrans). *USDA National Wildlife Research Center - Staff Publications*, USA. Paper 224.

Bellugi, U., Doyle, T., Korenberg, J., Masataka, N., & Zitzer-Comfort, C. (2007). *Nature and nurture: Williams syndrome across cultures*. Developmental Science. Retrieved from: http://dx.doi.org/10.1111/j.1467-7687.2007.00626.x April 2008

Bernstein, L. S. (1998). *Egregor*. The Rosicrucian Library Archive. Retrieved from: http://www.crcsite.org/egregor.htm June 2016

Boeree, C. G. (2006). *Carl Jung*. Personality Theories. Retrieved from: http://webspace.ship.edu/cgboer/jung.html September 2016

Boitani, L. & Ciucci, P. (1995). Comparative Social Ecology of Feral Dogs and Wolves. *Ethology Ecology & Evolution*, Vol. 7, No. 1, pp. 49-72. DOI: 10.1080/08927014.1995.9522969

Bostrom, N. (2003). Are You Living in a Computer Simulation? *Philosophical Quarterly*, Vol. 53, No. 211, pp. 243-255. DOI: n/a.

Bowlby, J. (1969), *Attachment and loss, Vol. 1: Attachment*. New York, NY: Basic Books.

———. (1973). *Attachment and loss, Vol. 2: Separation*. New York, NY: Basic Books.

———. (1980). *Attachment and loss, Vol. 3: Loss, sadness and depression*. New York, NY: Basic Books.

———. (1988a). *A Secure Base: Clinical Applications of Attachment Theory*. London, UK: Routledge.

———. (1988b). *A secure base: Parent-child attachment and healthy human development*.

Bowlby, J. & Ainsworth, M. (1969). Attachment Theory. *Human Evolution*, pp.1-25. DOI: 10.1080/14616730701711540

Boyd, D., Bee, H., & Johnson, P. (2009). *Lifespan development* (3rd Canadian Edition). Toronto, Ontario: Pearson.

Bretherton, I. (1992). The origin of attachment theory: John Bowlby and Mary Ainsworth. *Developmental Psychology*, Vol. 28, No. 5, pp. 759-775. DOI: 10.1037/0012-1649.28.5.759

Brown, K. 2017. Dalai Lama: Spirituality Without Quantum Physics Is an Incomplete Picture of Reality. Retrieved from: http://www.collective-evolution.com/2017/04/26/dalai-lama-spirituality-without-quantum-physics-is-an-incomplete-picture-of-reality/

Burger, J. M., & Cooper, H. M. (1979). The desirability of control. *Motivation and Emotion*, Vol. 3, No. 4, pp. 381-393. DOI: n/a

Carlson, D.A. (2008). Reproductive Biology of the Coyote (Canis latrans): Integration of Behavior and Physiology. Utah State University, USA. *Graduate Theses and Dissertations*.

Chance, P. (2008). *Learning and Behaviour* (6th Edition). Belmont, CA: Wadsworth.Chopra, D. (2008). *The Mirror of Relationships: Using Relationships to Transform Consciousness*. Knol. Retrieved from: http://knol.google.com/k/deepak-chopra/the-mirror-of-relationships/2ci5wkz6ok13p/3

Cimarelli, G., Turcsán, B., Bánlaki, Z., Range, F., & Virányi, Z. (2016). Dog Owners' Interaction Styles: Their Components and Associations with Reactions of Pet Dogs to a Social Threat. *Frontiers in Psychology*, Vol.7, No. 1979, DOI: 10.3389/fpsyg.2016.01979

Cimarelli, G., Turcsán, B., Range, F., & Virányi, Z. (2017). The Other End of the Leash: An Experimental Test to Analyze How Owners Interact with Their Pet Dogs. *Journal of Visualized Experiments*, Vol. 1, No. 128, pp. 1-11. DOI: doi:10.3791/56233

Clear Light Arts, ADL. (2008). *The Mirror of Relationship*. Heart & Soul Healing. Retrieved from: http://www.kenpage.com/mchnewsletter/0705mirror_relationship.html April 2010

Coile, C. (2005). *Bringing Dog Vision Into Focus*. Working Dogs Cyberzine. Retrieved from: http://www.workingdogs.com/vision_coile.htm December 2006

Coppinger, R. & Coppinger, L. (2001). *Dogs: A startling new understanding of canine origin, behaviour, & evolution*. New York, NY: Scribner.

———. (2016). *What is a dog?* Chicago, Il: University of Chicago Press.

Coppinger, R. & Feinstein, M. (2015). *How dogs work*. Chicago, Il: University of Chicago Press.

Darwin, C. (1859). *The Origin of Species by means of Natural Selection*. London, England: John Murray.

———. (1872). *The Expression of Emotions in Man and Animals*. London, England: John Murray.

Dickinson, E. (1924). *The Complete Poems*. Boston: Little, Brown.

Donatelle, R. J. & Thompson, A. M. (2011). *Health the Basics* (5th Edition). Toronto, Canada: Pearson.

Dongier, M. (2002). *Le Cerveau à Tous Les Niveaux*. Instituts de Recherche en Santé du Canada. Retrieved from: http://lecerveau.mcgill.ca/flash/index_d.html March 2007

Encyclopædia Britannica. (1998). *Madhyamika*. Encyclopædia Britannica, Inc. Retrieved from https://www.britannica.com/topic/Madhyamika December 2017

Erikson, E. H. (1980). *Identity and the life cycle*. New York, NY, US: W W Norton & Co.

Farndon, J., Woolf, A., Rooney A. & Gogerly, L. (2005). *The Great Scientists*. Toronto, Canada: Capella.

Fiset, S. (2007). Landmark-Based Search Memory in the Domestic Dog (Canis familiaris). *Journal of Comparative Psychology*, Vol. 121, No. 4, pp. 345-353. DOI: 10.1037/0735-7036.121.4.345

———. (2010). Differential Sensitivity to Human Communication in Dogs, Wolves, and Human Infants. *Science*, Vol. 329, No. 5988, pp. 142. DOI: 10.1126/science.1184045.

Folger, T. (2004). Einstein's Grand Quest for a Unified Theory. *Discover Magazine*, Special Einstein Issue.

Frank, H. & Gialdini-Frank, M. (1982). On the Effects of Domestication on Canine Social Development and Behavior. Elsevier Scientific Publishing Company, Amsterdam: *Applied Animal Ethology*, Vol. 8, No. 2, pp. 507-525. DOI: n/a

Freedman, D. G., King, J. A. & Elliot, O. (1961). Critical Period in the Social Development of Dogs. *American Association for the Advancement of Science*, Vol. 133, No. 3457, pp. 1016-1017. DOI: n/a

Freud, A. (1937). *The Ego and the Mechanisms of Defense* (revised edition: 1966). London, England: Hogarth Press and Institute of Psycho-Analysis.

Freud, S. (1923). *The Ego and the Id*. Mineola, NY: Dover Publications Inc.

Fugazza, C. (2014). Social learning and imitation in dogs (Canis familiaris). *Doctoral Thesis*, pp. 1–108. DOI: n/a

Fugazza, C., & Miklósi, Á. (2015). Social learning in dog training: The effectiveness of the Do as I do method compared to shaping/clicker training. *Applied Animal Behaviour Science*, Vol. 171, pp. 146–151. DOI: 10.1016/j.applanim.2015.08.033

Fugazza, C., Pógány, A., & Miklósi, A. (2016). Recall of Others' Actions after Incidental Encoding Reveals Episodic-like Memory in Dogs. *Current Biology*, Vol. 26, No. 23, pp. 3209-3213. DOI: 10.1016/j.cub.2016.09.057

Gallese, V., Gernsbacher, M. A., Heyes, C., Hickok, G., & Iacoboni, M. (2011). Mirror Neuron Forum. *Perspectives on Psychological Science*, Vol. 6, No. 4, pp. 369–407. DOI: 10.1177/1745691611413392

Grandin, T. & Johnson, C. (2005). *Animals in Translation: Using the Mysteries of Autism to Decode Animal Behaviour*. New York, NY: Scribner.

Greene, B. (2003). *The Elegant Universe*. New York, NY: W.W. Norton & Company.

Grobstein, P. & Cyckowski, L. (2009). *Brain and Behaviour*. Serendip. Retrieved from: http://serendip.brynmawr.edu/bb February 2007

Groleau, R. (2003). *The Elegant Universe*. PBS. Retrieved from: http://www.pbs.org/wgbh/nova/elegant/dimensions.html January 2007

Guo, K., Meints, K., Hall, S., Hall, S. & Mills, D. (2009). Left Gaze Bias in Humans, Rhesus Monkeys and Domestic Dogs. *Animal Cognition*, Vol. 12, pp. 409-418. DOI: 10.1007/s10071-008-0199-3

Hare, B. & Woods, V. (2013). *The Genius of Dogs: How Dogs Are Smarter Than You Think*. New York, NY: Plume.

Hart, G. (1986). *Dictionary of Egyptian gods and goddesses*. New York, NY: Routledge

Herschel, J. (1972). A Scaled Ratio of Body Weight to Brain Weight as a Comparative Index for Relative Importance of Brain Size in Mammals of Widely Varying Body Mass. *Psychological Reports*, Vol. 31, pp. 84-86. DOI: 10.2466/pr0.1972.31.1.84

Hill, J. (2010). *Ancient Egypt gods: The Aten*. Ancient Egypt on Line. Retrieved from http://www.ancientegyptonline.co.uk/amarnareligion.htm 1 April 2014

Huber, A., Barber, L. A., Faragó, T., Corsin, M. A., & Huber, L. (2017). Investigating emotional contagion in dogs (Canis familiaris) to emotional sounds of humans and conspecific. *Animal Cognition*, Vol. 20, No. 4, pp. 703-715. DOI: 10.1007/s10071-017-1092-8

Hughes, P. & Riordan, D. (2017). *Dynamic Psychotherapy Explained* (2nd Edition). Boca Raton, FL: CRC Press.

Hugo, T. (1853). *A Memoir of Gundulf, Bishop of Rochester. Library St-Michael's College*. London, UK: Lincoln's-Inn Fields.

Insel, T. & Young, L. (1999). *Social Behaviour Transformed With One New Gene*. Science Daily. Emory University Health Sciences Center. Retrieved from: http://www.sciencedaily.com/releases/1999/08/990819070117.htm

Ivancevic, V. G. & Ivancevic, T. T. (2007). *Applied Differential Geometry: A Modern Introduction*. Singapore: World Scientific Publishing Co.

Isaacson, W. (2008). *Einstein: His Life and Universe*. New York, NY: Simon & Schuster.

Jung, C. G. (1936). The Concept of the Collective Unconsciousness. *Journal of St-Bartholomew's Hospital*, Vol. 44, pp.37. DOI: n/a

───. (1959). *The Archetypes and the Collective Unconscious* (2nd Edition). New York, NY: Routledge.

Kazlev, A. (2003). *The Triune Brain*. Kheper. Retrieved from: http://www.kheper.net/topics/intelligence/MacLean.htm March 2013

Kis, A., Szakadát, S., Gácsi, M., Kovács, E., Simor, P., Török, C., Gombos, F., Bódizs, R., & Topál, J. (2017). The interrelated effect of sleep and learning in dogs (Canis familiaris); an EEG and behavioural study. *Scientific Report*. Vol.7, No. 41873, pp. 1-6. DOI: 10.1038/srep41873

Kroger, J. (1996). *Identity in Adolescence: The Balance Between Self and Others* (2nd Edition). New York, NY: Routledge.

Kubinyi, E., Virányi, Z. & Miklósi, Á. (2007). Comparative Cognition and Behaviour Reviews. *Doctoral thesis*. Budapest: Eötvös University.

Languirand, J. & Proulx, J. (2008). *Le Dieu Cosmique; À la Recherche du Dieu d'Einstein*. Montreal, Canada: Le Jour.

Lesch, K.-P., Araragi, N., Waider, J., van den Hove, D. & Gutknecht, L. (2012). Targeting brain serotonin synthesis: insights into neurodevelopmental disorders with long-term outcomes related to negative emotionality, aggression and antisocial behaviour. *Philosophical Transactions of the Royal Society B: Biological Sciences*, Vol. 367, No. 1601, pp. 2426-2443 DOI: 10.1098/rstb.2012.0039

Lewis, S. (Director) & Veritasium (Producer). (2015). *Quantum Entanglement & Spooky Action at a Distance*. [Video]. Retrieved from https://www.youtube.com/watch?v=ZuvK-od647c&t=5s October 2017

Lorenz, K. (1954). *Man Meets Dog.* New York, NY: Routledge

———. (1961). *King Solomon's Ring.* London, England: Methuen Publishing.

McGill University. (2016). *The Brain From Top to Bottom.* Retrieved from http://thebrain.mcgill.ca/intermediaire.php September 2016

McRae, M. (2017). *This Crazy Twist on Black Holes Says There Was No Big Bang We could be living in a bouncy Universe.* Science Alert. Retrieved from https://sciencealert.com/regular-black-holes-model-eliminate-singularity-big-bang November 2017

Miklósi, A., Topál, J., & Csányi, V. (2004). Comparative social cognition: What can dogs teach us? *Animal Behaviour,* Vol. 67, No. 6, pp 995–1004. DOI: 10.1016/j.anbehav.2003.10.008

Mosby's medical dictionary. (2013). (9th ed.). St. Louis, MO: Mosby Elsevier

Molenberghs, P., Cunnington, R., & Mattingley, J. B. (2009). Is the mirror neuron system involved in imitation? A short review and meta-analysis. *Neuroscience and Biobehavioral Reviews*, Vol. 33, No. 7, pp. 975–980. DOI: 10.1016/j.neubiorev.2009.03.010

Moons, C. (2016). Canine Behaviour and Genetics: Special issue on the London 2015 meetings. *Journal of Veterinary Behavior,* Vol. 16, pp.1-3 DOI: 10.1016/j.jveb.2016.12.001

Morenz, S. (1973). *Egyptian Religion.* Ithaca, NY: Cornell University Press.

Mosby's Medical Dictionary. (2017). Mindfulness meditation. (n.d.) Mosby's Medical Dictionary, 8th edition. Retrieved from http://medical-dictionary.thefreedictionary.com/mindfulness+meditation August 2017

Nagasawa, M., Mogi, K., & Kikusui, T. (2009). Attachment between humans and dogs. *Japanese Psychological Research*, Vol. 51, No. 3, pp. 209–221. DOI: 10.1111/j.1468-5884.2009.00402.x

National Human Genome Research Institute. (1997). *Dishevelled-1 Knockout Mice*. National Institutes of Health. Retrieved from: http://www.genome.gov/10000668 February 2007

Neves, J. C. S. (2017). Bouncing cosmology inspired by regular black holes. *General Relativity Gravitation*, Vol. 49, No. 124. DOI: 10.1007/s10714-017-2288-6

New York, NY: Basic Books.

New York Times. (1955). Obituary for Albert Einstein. 19 April.

Online Etymology Dictionary. (2017). *Adolescence and adulthood etymologic definitions*. Retrieved from https://www.etymonline.com December 2017

Ortolani, A., Vernooij, H. & Coppinger, R. (2008). Ethiopian Village Dogs: Behavioural Responses to a Stranger's Approach. *Applied Animal Behaviour Science,* Vol. 119, No. 3-4, pp. 202-218. DOI: 10.1016/j.applanim.2009.03.011

Overall, K. (1997). *Clinical Behavioural Medicine for Small Animals*. St-Louis, MO: Mosby.

Pal, S. K. (2011). Mating System of Free-Ranging Dogs (Canis familiaris). *International Journal of Zoology*, Vol. 713, pp. 130. DOI: 10.1155/2011/314216

Persson, M. E., Roth, L. S. V, Johnsson, M., Wright, D., & Jensen, P. (2015). Human-directed social behaviour in dogs shows significant heritability. *Genes, Brain and Behavior*, Vol. 14, No. 4, pp. 337–344. DOI: 10.1111/gbb.12194

Pierre, M. J. (2006). *Superstring!* Retrieved from: tttp://www.sukidog.com/jpierre/strings/why.htm March 2015

Rees, C. (2012). Children's attachments. *Paediatrics and Child Health*, Vol. 22, No. 5, pp. 186-192. DOI: 10.1016/j.paed.2011.10.001

Renard, G. (2004). *Disappearance of the Universe*. Carlsbad, CA: Hay House.

———. (2006). *Your Immortal Reality*. Carlsbad, CA: Hay House.

Rizzolatti, G. (2005). The mirror neuron system and its function in humans. *Anatomy and Embryology*, Vol. 210, No. 5-6, pp. 419-421. DOI: 10.1007/s00429-005-0039-z

Rizzolatti, G., & Craighero, L. (2004). The mirror-neuron system. *Annual Review of Neuroscience*, Vol. 27, No. 1, pp. 169–192. DOI: 10.1146/annurev.neuro.27.070203.144230

Rizzolatti, G., & Fabbri-Destro, M. (2008). The mirror system and its role in social cognition. *Current Opinion in Neurobiology*, Vol. 18, No. 2, pp. 179–184. DOI: 10.1016/j.conb.2008.08.001

Rosenstock, I. M., Strecher, V. J., & Becker, M. H. (1988). Social learning theory and the health belief model. *Health Education Quarterly*, Vol. 15, No. 2, pp.175-183. DOI: 10.1177/109019818801500203

Rugaas, T. (1996). *On Talking Terms With Dogs: Calming Signals*. Carlsborg, WA: Legacy By Mail.

———. (2005). Calming Signals: What Your Dog Tells You. [Educational DVD]. United-States: Dogwise Publishing.

Ruiz-Izaguirre, E., Eilers, C. H. A. M., Bokkers, E. A. M., Ortolani, A., & Ortega-Pachecho, A. (2011). Village Dogs at the Pacific Coast of Mexico: Socialization towards Humans and Human-Dog Interactions. *Journal of Veterinary Behavior*, Vol. 6, No. 1, pp.66. DOI: 10.1016/j.jveb.2010.09.042

Schacter, D. L., Gilbert, D. T., Wegner, D. M., & Nock, M. K. (2015). *Introducing Psychology* (3rd Edition). New York, NY: Macmillan Publishers.

Scott, J. P. & Fuller, J. L. (1965). *Genetics and Social Behaviour of the Dog*. Chicago, IL The University of Chicago Press.

Sheldrake, R. (1999). *Dogs That Know When Their Owners Are Coming Home, and other unexplained powers of animals*. New York, NY: Three Rivers Press.

———. (2005). *Morphic Fields and Morphic Resonance: An Introduction*. Retrieved from: https://www.sheldrake.org/research/morphic-resonance/introduction

Schucman, H. [scribe]. (2007). *A Course in Miracles* (3rd Edition). Mill Valley, CA: Foundation for Inner Peace.

Siegel, A., Roeling, T. A. P., Gregg, T. R. & Kruk, M. R. (1999). Neuropharmacology of brain-stimulation-evoked aggression. *Neuroscience and Biobehavioral Reviews*, Vol. 7634, pp. 359-389. DOI: 10.1016/S0149-7634(98)00040-2

Silver, J. (Producer), Wachowski Brothers (Director). (1999). *The Matrix*. [Motion picture]. United-States: Warner Bros.

Skinner, E. A. (1996). A guide to constructs of control. *Journal of Personality and Social Psychology*, Vol. 71, No. 3, pp. 549-570. DOI: 10.1037/0022-3514.71.3.549

Stanley, D. G. (2007). Ecology of Coyotes in Urban Landscape. *School of Environment and Natural Resources*, Ohio State University, Columbus, OH, and Max McGraw Wildlife Foundation, Dundee, IL, USA.

Stavrinos, D., Byington, K.W. & Schwebel, D.C. (2009). Effect of Cell Phone Distraction on Pediatric Pedestrian Injury Risk. *Pediatrics Journal*, Vol. 123, No. 2, pp. 179-185. DOI: 10.1542/peds.2008-1382

Teglas, E., Gergely, A., Kupan, K., Miklósi, A., & Topál, J. (2012). Dogs' Gaze Following Is Tuned to Human Communicative Signals. *Current Biology*, Vol. 22, No. 3, pp. 209-212. DOI: 10.1016/j.cub.2011.12.018

Topál, J., Miklósi, A., Csányi, V., & Dóka, A. (1998). Attachment Behavior in Dogs (Canis familiaris): A New Application of Ainsworth's (1969) Strange Situation Test. *Journal of Comparative Psychology*, Vol. 112, No. 3, pp. 219-229. DOI: 10.1037/0735-7036.112.3.219

Tortora, G. J. & Grabowski, S.R. (2000). *Principles of Anatomy and Physiology*. Toronto, Ontario: John Wiley & Sons, Inc.

Virányi, Z., Gácsi, M., Kubinyi, E., Topál, J., Belényi, B., Ujfalussy, D. & Miklósi, A. (2008). Comprehension of Human Pointing Gestures in Young Human-reared Wolves (Canis lupus) and Dogs (Canis familiaris). *Animal Cognition*, Vol. 11, No. 3, pp. 373-387. DOI: 10.1007/s10071-007-0127-y

Walsch, N. D. (Ed.) (2005). *The Complete Conversations with god, an uncommon dialogue*. New York, NY: Putnam.

———. (2017). *Conversation with god, Book 4: Awaken the species*. Faber, VA: Rainbow Ridge.

Way, J. G., Szumylo, D.L.M. & Strauss, E.G. (2006). An Ethogram Developed on Captive Eastern Coyotes (Canis latrans). *Canadian Field-Naturalist*, Vol. 120, No. 3, pp. 263-288. DOI: 10.22621/cfn.v120i3.317

Wiersma, J. (2001). Maximum Estimated Bite Force, Skull Morphology, and Primary Prey Size in North American Carnivores. *School of Graduate Studies and Research*, Laurentian University of Sudbury, Ontario, Canada.

World Health Organization. (1993). Report of WHO Consultation on Dog Ecology Studies related to Rabies Control. Geneva: Ref. WHO/Rab.Res/93.42, Corr.1.

Wynne, D. L. (2009). How Well Do Wolves And Dogs Understand People? *North American Wildlife Park Foundation*, Inc. Wolf Park. Battle Ground, IN.

Zeanah, C. H. (1990). A Secure Base: Parent-Child Attachment and Healthy Human Development. *The Journal of Nervous and Mental Disease*, Vol. 178, No. 1, pp. 62. DOI: 10.1097/00005053-199001000-00017

Zentall, T. H. (2001). Imitation in Animals: Evidence, Function, and Mechanism. *Cybernetics and Systems: An International Journal*, Vol. 32, pp. 53-96. DOI: 10.1146/annurev.neuro.27.070203.144230

Zhang, Y., Agnew, M., Roger, T., Roux, F. S., Konrad, T, Faccio, D., Leach, J. & Forbes, A. (2017). Simultaneous entanglement swapping of multiple orbital angular momentum states of light. *Nature Communications*, Vol. 8, No.1, pp. 1-12. DOI: 10.1038/s41467-017-00706-1

Figure B. Albear

"The one thing we're all waiting for, is peace on earth - an end to war, it's a miracle we need - the miracle, the miracle we're all waiting for today."

— Queen, The Miracle, 1989

Author Bio

 Gaby Dufresne-Cyr is the founder, teacher, and senior animal trainer at the Dogue Shop where she teaches domestic and exotic animal training, social-cognitive learning theory, attachment, and exotic animal-assisted therapy as a means of enrichment, training, and conservation to future professionals.

Gaby is an animal behaviour consultant who devotes her time teaching the science behind animal training to her students and the general public. She conducts domestic and exotic animal-assisted therapy with at-risk teens in many high schools in Montreal.

Gaby is currently studying for a second degree in cognitive-neuroscience at Concordia University, Quebec, Canada, to deepen the human-animal bond. She also travels internationally to speak about the science of animal behaviour, inter-species attachment, social-cognitive animal training, and exotic animal-assisted therapy programs as effective therapeutic processes and behaviour modification strategies.

Figure C. Hariette
"As a man changes his own nature, so does the attitude of the world change towards him."
—Mahatma Gandhi